think pink scotland

D1326767

LADIES, HAVE YOU CHECKED YOUR CUPCAKES RECENTLY?

EARLY DIAGNOSIS OF BREAST CANCER COULD HELP TO SAVE YOUR RASPBERRY RIPPLES OR MORE IMPORTANTLY, YOUR LIFE.

THINKPINKSCOTLAND.ORG

FAIRY RECIPE

1 cup	Pink sugar
1 tsp	Mischief
1 sprinkle	Sweets
1 drop	Beauty
1 pinch	Butterfly wing dust
1 dash	Chocolate chip cookies

❶ Mix together in a rose bowl. ❷ Stir with a pixie sized wand. ❸ Leave until Halloween. ❹ Say the magic words 'Fly Away!'

Anna Guy, aged 9
Killearn

THE RECIPE FOR SUCCESS

The recipe for success
is what we all strive to find
some of us will get there
some will get left behind

but what we all have in common
by buying this wee book
is a need to show we care
even if we cannot cook

a whole lot of ingredients
have gone into making this book
so hopefully you will enjoy it
and maybe even learn to cook

as long as all who buy it
know it's for a fantastic cause
so tell everybody you know
even Santa Clause!!

more wee books can follow
so keep on spending your pounds
this could be your way
of helping good people stay around.

so thank you if you bought this book
and if you want another
you can find out where to get them
just check inside the cover.

Thank you

Lynn Henderson,
Glasgow

FOREWORD

THIS BOOK HAS BEEN PRODUCED TO HELP RAISE FUNDS FOR BREAST CANCER RESEARCH IN SCOTLAND.

All of the proceeds will be directed to the Beatson Translational Research Centre and no administration costs will be deducted.

We have loved producing this wonderful book and hope you enjoy trying out lots of the recipes included. We have been fortunate enough to have received contributions from a variety of well known household names including celebrity chefs, politicians, sports and TV personalities, local businesses and, of course, our closest friends and family.

Thank you for supporting Think Pink. Further copies of 'Think Pink's Fantastic Recipes for a Fantastic Cause' are available from thinkpinkscotland.org or telephone 0141 330 4951 or Borders Bookshop.

Lynn Murray, Freda Robertson, Ann Graham, Sharmi Musgrave and Roisin Munn

STARTERS

SMOKED MACKEREL PÂTÉ

Serves 4-6

4	Smoked mackerel fillets, skinned
225g	Cream cheese
1-2	Garlic cloves, finely chopped
2 tbsp	Fresh chives, chopped
1 tbsp	Worcester sauce
1	Lemon, juiced
	Salt
	Cayenne pepper
	Warmed Melba toast, to serve

❶ Break up the mackerel and put in a food processor. Add the cream cheese, garlic, lemon juice and herbs. ❷ Process the mixture until fairly smooth and add Worcester sauce, salt and cayenne pepper to taste. ❸ Whizz to mix, then spoon the pâté into a dish, cover with cling film, and chill. ❹ Garnish with chives and serve with Melba toast.

Note: Herbs can be substituted with parsley or chervil and fish can be replaced with peppered mackerel, smoked haddock or kipper fillets.

Fiona Fox
Buchanan Castle, Drymen

TUNA PÂTÉ
WITH PRAWNS

Serves 4-6

2 x 198g	Tins of tuna, drained
125g	(4oz) Butter, melted
15ml	(1 tbsp) Lemon juice
200g	Cooked prawns, defrosted
225g	Full fat soft cheese
50g	(2oz) Fresh white breadcrumbs
125g	(4oz) Butter, melted
	Freshly ground pepper

❶ Place tuna, soft cheese, melted butter (4oz), breadcrumbs, lemon juice and seasoning in a food processor and blend. ❷ Chop prawns roughly and stir into the mixture. Season to taste. ❸ Spread into ramekin dishes or a terrine dish. At this point you can freeze the recipe if you wish. ❹ Otherwise continue and pour the remaining 4oz of melted butter over the mixture.

Ali Thompson
Buchanan Castle, Drymen

DOUBLE SALMON TERRINE

Makes 12-15 servings

2	Small tins of salmon, drained
250g	Smoked salmon, diced
2 tbsp	Fresh parsley, chopped
3	Spring onions, sliced
1 tsp	Dried tarragon
125ml	Softened butter
125ml	Mayonnaise
15ml	Dijon mustard
15ml	Lemon juice
½ tsp	Black pepper

❶ Flake salmon, discard skin and bones. ❷ Gently combine flaked and smoked salmon, parsley, onions and tarragon. ❸ In a separate bowl, beat together butter, mayonnaise, mustard, lemon juice and pepper then add salmon mixture and gently combine. ❹ Line an 8x4 inch (1½ litre) loaf tin with plastic wrap, spoon in salmon mixture and cover with plastic wrap. ❺ Refrigerate for about 3 hours or until firm. ❻ Unmould and serve in slices.

This is the easiest and most impressive starter or buffet dish I have ever come across.

Ann McGeechan

AUSTRALIAN SALMON MOUSSE

Serves 6 (or 4 as main course)

16oz	Tin of red salmon, drained with bones and skin removed	¼ cup	Stuffed olives, chopped
½ cup	Cold water	2 tsp	Onion, grated
1 cup	Mayonnaise	1 tbsp	Lemon juice or mild vinegar
1 tbsp	Gelatine	1 tsp	Bottled horseradish
½ cup	Celery, finely diced		Pinch salt
		¼ tsp	Paprika
		1 cup	Sour cream

❶ Soak gelatine in cold water, heat to dissolve if necessary and stir into mayonnaise. ❷ Flake and mash salmon and add other ingredients, blending well. ❸ Pour into lightly oiled fish-shaped mould. Chill until firm. ❹ Serve as first course or luncheon main course.

Mousse is very tasty and pink – a family favourite.

Rhona Nicol
Australia

SMOKED HADDOCK FISHCAKES

Serves 4 (2-3 as main course)

1lb	Smoked haddock, skinned and boned
1 tbsp	Lemon juice
1	Long red chilli, seeded and finely chopped
3 tbsp	Coriander, finely chopped
4	Spring onions
½lb	Mashed potato
2	Eggs
	Flour
8oz	Breadcrumbs
	Salt and pepper

❶ Cook the fish sprinkled with the lemon juice in the oven on a moderate heat for 8 minutes or microwave for 3 minutes. ❷ Flake when cool and mix together with the potato, coriander, spring onions, chilli and salt and pepper. ❸ With floured hands, shape into patties and freeze for a couple of hours. ❹ To finish the fishcakes off dust them in flour, dip into beaten egg and then roll in the breadcrumbs. At this stage you can freeze them or cook them straight away. (I like to shallow fry them in olive oil).

Audrey

THAI FISH CAKES WITH SWEET AND SOUR DIPPING SAUCE

Serves 4-6 (makes approximately 16-20 fishcakes)

Fishcakes:

700g	Skinless white fish fillets, cut into chunks
1½ tbsp	Fish sauce
1½ tbsp	Red curry paste
2-3	Kaffir lime leaves or lime zest, finely shredded
1	Egg
2 tbsp	Palm or muscovado sugar
1 tsp	Salt
60g	Green beans, thinly sliced
	Groundnut or sunflower oil for shallow frying

Dipping sauce:

50ml	White wine vinegar
100ml	Caster sugar
1 tbsp	Water
3 tsp	Fish sauce
50g	Cucumber, diced very finely
25g	Carrot, diced very finely
25g	Red onion, chopped very finely
2	Bird's eye chillies (or to taste), sliced very thinly

❶ For the sauce, gently heat the vinegar, sugar and water in a small pan until the sugar has dissolved. Turn up heat, bring to the boil for 1 minute, remove from heat and leave to cool. ❷ When cool, stir in the fish sauce, cucumber, carrot, onion and chillies. (There should be enough chopped vegetables in the liquid to form a thick sauce.) Set aside. ❸ For the fish cakes, put all the ingredients, except the green beans, in a food processor. Combine until smooth, then stir in the sliced green beans. ❹ Divide the mixture into equal pieces. Roll each one into a ball and then flatten into a disc about 6cm/2½ inch in diameter. ❺ Heat the oil in a large frying pan and shallow fry the fish cakes in batches for 1 minute on each side, until golden brown. Serve with the dipping sauce.

After Stage 4, can be frozen, uncooked.

Sharmi Musgrave
Buchanan Castle, Drymen

CHRISTINE'S SALMON MOUSSE

½ cup	Double cream
1 tbsp	(1 sheet) Gelatine
¼ cup	Cold water
½ cup	Boiling water
½ cup	Mayonnaise
1 tbsp	Lemon juice
1½ tbsp	Onion, grated
½ tsp	Tabasco
1 tsp	Salt
2 cups	Salmon
2 tsp	Capers, finely chopped
½ tsp	Paprika

❶ Sprinkle gelatine over the cold water in a bowl. Leave to stand and soften for 5 minutes. Pour the boiling water over this and mix well with a wire whisk. ❷ Let cool to room temperature then add the mayonnaise, lemon juice, paprika, tabasco, onion, salt and mix well. ❸ Add the capers and salmon and mix again. ❹ Fold in the cream and pour the mixture into an oiled fish mould. ❺ Place the mould in the fridge for several hours until set.

To unmould, loosen around the edge with the tip of a knife. Dip chilled mould quickly in a basin of hot water up to rim and then turn out onto a serving plate. Garnish with lemon wedges and parsley and serve with thinly sliced brown bread or Melba toast.

Christine Gastall
Drymen

TERRINE OF CHICKEN AND PORK

Serves 6-8

1lb	Pigs liver, minced	4 tbsp	Brandy
1lb	Lean pork	2	Eggs, beaten
1lb	Pork sausage meat	½ tsp	Ground nutmeg
2	Medium onions, peeled and chopped	16	Rashers of streaky bacon
2oz	Butter	4	Chicken breasts
2 tbsp	Parsley, chopped	4	Bay leaves
4oz	Soft white breadcrumbs		Salt and pepper

❶ Mix together liver, pork and sausage meat. ❷ Fry onion in butter until soft. ❸ Mix all ingredients except bacon, chicken and bay leaves. ❹ Stretch the bacon and line a deep dish with some of them. Add half of the stuffing mixture and spread evenly. ❺ Beat the chicken breasts to flatten, place in tin or dish, cover with stuffing mixture and top with bacon and bay leaves. ❻ Cover with foil and place in a roasting tin half filled with warm water. ❼ Cook for about 4 hours at 325°F. ❽ When cooked, place weights on top of foil (to press down contents really well to arrive at a layered effect). Cool slowly.

This is a luxurious dish for summer salad days and for rather special occasions such as at a buffet table.

Val MacDonald
Drymen

CHEESY LEEK AND BACON BAKE

Serves 4

1   **Leek**
Pancetta or bacon, diced
St Agur Cheese
Cream

❶ Finely dice the root end of the leek and layer into each of 4 ramekins.
❷ Add chopped pancetta or bacon and chopped St Agur Cheese. It must be St Agur as you only need a little, and it melts beautifully. ❸ Add another layer of leeks and bacon. ❹ Top up to about 1cm from the top with double cream and bake for 10 minutes until bubbling. Serve with homemade bread for dunking.

Laura E. Alexander
West Kilbride

DOLMADES

Serves 6

1	Packet of vine leaves
500g	Pork mince
½ cup	Basmati rice
1 tbsp	Parsley, chopped
1 tsp	Cinnamon
1 tsp	Dried mint
½ tsp	Ground black pepper
1 tsp	Salt
1 tbsp	Tomato purée
1	Lemon, juiced
2 tbsp	Olive oil
1	Onion, chopped

❶ Separate vine leaves and place in a pot of boiling water. Bring back to the boil, remove from heat and leave for 1 minute. Drain vine leaves in a colander. ❷ Meanwhile use a large bowl to mix all the ingredients together using your hands. ❸ Separate your leaves and place them on a clean surface right side face down. ❹ Place a heaped spoonful of the mixture in the middle of each vine leaf. ❺ Take the bottom end of the leaf and fold on top of the mixture and roll up half way. ❻ Fold in the sides and continue rolling into a neat parcel. ❼ Place the vine leaves leaf end down to avoid bursting in a medium sized pot. Place them round the pot in a circle, making your way into the centre and onto the next layer. Pack neatly, but not too tightly. ❽ Place 2 side plates on top of Dolmades upside down. Just cover plates with boiling water. ❾ Bring back to the boil and cook on low heat for 1 hour. Serve with a wedge of lemon and a side salad.

They are also delicious with a Neapolitan sauce.
This is one of my Dad's favourite recipes.

Simone Antoniou Fairfull
Killearn

SOUPS

CREAMY BUTTERNUT SQUASH AND RED PEPPER SOUP

Serves 4

1oz	(25g) Butter
1	Large onion, chopped
1	Butternut squash, peeled, deseeded and chopped
1	Red pepper
1 pt	Stock
7oz	(200g) Cream cheese
½ pt	Milk
2 tbsp	Chives, chopped
	Salt and pepper

❶ Melt the butter in a large saucepan, add onions and fry gently until softened.
❷ Add butternut squash, red pepper and stock; simmer for 20 minutes until vegetables are soft. ❸ Add half the cream cheese and liquidise the mixture.
❹ In the saucepan, add milk and half the chives and season. ❺ Ladle soup into bowls, top with dollop of cream cheese and sprinkle with chives and ground black pepper.

Susan McKenzie
Balfron

BUTTERNUT SQUASH SOUP WITH GINGER AND CORIANDER

Serves 4-6

1kg	Butternut squash, peeled and cubed
3 tbsp	Olive oil
	Salt
	Freshly ground pepper
	Bunch coriander, chopped (including stalks)
	Garlic cloves, chopped
5cm	Ginger, peeled and grated
1	Red chilli, deseeded and chopped
1	Onion, finely chopped
2	Sticks celery, chopped
500ml	Vegetable stock
400ml	Coconut cream
1	Lime, juiced
	Chilli and coriander to garnish

❶ Coat squash in 2 tbsp olive oil and roast at 200°C/400°F/Gas Mark 6 for 15-20 minutes until caramelised and check seasoning. ❷ Heat 1 tablespoon of oil and add handful coriander, garlic, ginger, chilli and cook for 2 minutes. ❸ Add onion and celery and simmer gently for 10 minutes to soften. ❹ Add stock and coconut cream, bring to the boil, then simmer for 10 minutes. ❺ Add roasted squash and cook gently for a few minutes. ❻ Liquidise until smooth. ❼ Add some coriander leaves and the lime juice. Serve garnished with some chopped chilli and lime zest.

I generally have some extra chilli for those who want even more kick.

Elaine Robertson
Glasgow

SPICY RED PEPPER SOUP

Serves 4-6

1 tbsp	Oil	2	Large tomatoes, peeled and sliced (or tin of chopped tomatoes)
1	Large onion, chopped		
2	Garlic cloves, crushed		
3	Large red peppers, seeded, cored and chopped	1	Small chilli pepper, deseeded and chopped (vary amount to suit)
1	Medium potato, peeled and diced	1¾ pts	Stock
2 tbsp	Tomato puree		Salt and pepper

❶ Heat oil in pan and soften onion, add garlic and stir well. ❷ Stir in the peppers, tomato puree, potato, tomatoes and stock. ❸ Add seasoning, bring to the boil and simmer for 30 minutes. ❹ Reserve 2 spoonfuls of peppers, liquidise soup then stir in reserved peppers. ❺ Adjust seasoning and serve with swirls of plain, unsweetened yoghurt and sprigs of chervil or parsley.

Susan McKenzie
Balfron

SWEET POTATO SOUP

Serves 10

2 tbsp	Olive oil
2lb	Sweet potatoes
2	Large onions, chopped
1	Large clove garlic, peeled
½	Red chilli, seeds removed
3 pts	Chicken stock
½	Tin of reduced fat coconut milk (other half can be placed in small container and frozen)

❶ Cook onion and garlic in oil until soft and transparent. ❷ Add sweet potato, chilli and continue 'sweating' for a few minutes (stirring to prevent sticking). ❸ Add stock and simmer covered until vegetables are soft. ❹ Allow to cool slightly. Add coconut milk and blend with a hand blender. Serve garnished with some fresh coriander.

Julie Briggs
Drymen

SPANISH GARLIC SOUP (SOPA DE AJO)

Serves 2

5	Cloves of garlic, peeled and thinly sliced
1 tsp	Paprika (Spanish if possible)
3	Handfuls stale bread, cut into bite size chunks
1 litre	Boiling water
2	Eggs, beaten
	Olive oil
	Salt to taste

❶ Heat the oil in a saucepan and gently fry the garlic until it turns golden brown.
❷ Add the paprika, stir, and immediately add the boiling water (it burns easily).
❸ Add the bread and let it boil for a few minutes until it is soft. ❹ Add the beaten eggs and stir vigorously. Add salt to taste.

As a variation, you can add a couple of spoonfuls of Spanish cured ham (jamón) cut into small cubes.

Eve Hampton
Madrid

SPINACH AND ORANGE SOUP

Serves 4

50g Butter
25g Flour
1 Onion, finely chopped
250g Spinach, washed and
roughly shredded
750ml Chicken stock
2 Oranges
¼ tsp Nutmeg
Salt and pepper

❶ Melt butter, add onion and cook until soft. Stir in flour and cook for 1-2 minutes. ❷ Add stock, a little at a time and bring to the boil. ❸ Stir in spinach, orange segments, nutmeg and seasoning, bring to the boil and simmer for 10-15 minutes. ❹ Liquidise until smooth.

Wendi Bates
Balfron

RAYMOND'S LENTIL SOUP

Serves 4

75g	Smoked bacon or pancetta
225g	Onions
225g	Carrots
175g	Celery
275g	Lentils
1½ pts	Chicken stock
1	Bay leaf
½ tsp	Dried thyme

❶ Fry bacon, onions, carrots and celery in a lug of olive oil. ❷ Add the lentils, stir in the stock, bay leaf, thyme and then season to taste. ❸ Bring to the boil, cover pan and simmer for 45-60 minutes or until lentils are soft.

Raymond McHugh
Glasgow

GREEN VEGGIE SOUP

Serves 4

60ml	Olive oil
1	Onion, finely chopped
2	Garlic cloves, crushed
1	Celery stick, chopped
1	Courgette, chopped
1	Head of broccoli, chopped
1¾ litre	Vegetable stock
150g	Frozen green peas
80g	Frozen soya beans
85g	Baby spinach leaves, torn into pieces
2 tbsp	Hemp oil

❶ Heat the olive oil in a large saucepan and cook the onion, garlic and celery until lightly browned. ❷ Add the courgette and broccoli and cook for a further 5 minutes. Pour in the stock and bring to the boil. ❸ Simmer for 5 minutes and add the peas, soya beans and spinach. Continue to simmer for 5-10 minutes until the vegetables are tender and check seasoning. ❹ Once served into bowls, drizzle the hemp oil on top.

This soup is very nutritious and can be adapted to include any vegetable that you like. It is lovely served with some soda bread. For extra taste, season with a dollop of pesto.

Jacqui Crawford
Glasgow

PEA SOUP

Serves 4

907g	Frozen peas
1 litre	Chicken stock
2	Onions, chopped
1 tsp	Curry powder or paste
	Tub low-fat crème fraîche
	Salt and pepper

❶ Fry the chopped onions in some butter and olive oil until soft. ❷ Add the curry powder or paste and mix well. ❸ Add the chicken stock and frozen peas. ❹ Cook for 30 minutes or so and then puree with a hand blender. ❺ Add crème fraîche and serve up with some nice bread.

Really tasty soup.

Rhona Baxter
Aberdeen

FRENCH ONION SOUP

Serves 4

3-4 **Good sized onions, sliced into rings and halved**
2 pts **Chicken stock**
Grated cheese
Olive oil
Salt and pepper
Splash of brandy (optional)

❶ Brown the onions in a little olive oil. ❷ Add the stock and brandy if desired and simmer gently until the onions are soft. ❸ Season and once served into bowls, top with some croutons and grated cheese.

Gillian Guthrie
Bearsden

LETTUCE SOUP

Serves 4-6

1	Large lettuce
1oz	Butter
1	Onion
1	Potato
4oz	Streaky bacon
2 pts	Chicken stock
	Salt and pepper

❶ Sauté the onion and diced bacon in butter, until soft. ❷ Add shredded lettuce and grated potato. ❸ Add a small amount of stock and simmer for 30 minutes. ❹ When everything is cooked through, liquidise. ❺ Put soup back in the pan and add more stock and seasoning to taste. Serve with croutons.

Betty Twaddle
Balmaha

EASY MUSHROOM SOUP

Serves 4

8oz	Mushrooms (large black are best)
1oz	Garlic
2	Sprigs of parsley
2oz	Butter
2 pts	Chicken or veal stock (homemade is best)
	Nutmeg
	Salt and pepper
2	Thick slices of bread
2fl oz	Double cream
	Parsley, chopped

❶ Wipe the mushrooms and chop the garlic finely. Pull the leaves off the parsley and discard the stalks. ❷ In a large saucepan, melt the butter over a low heat. Tear the mushrooms into pieces and add to the butter. Increase the heat and stir until the juices come freely from the mushrooms. ❸ Add the stock, garlic, parsley, a little grated nutmeg, salt and pepper and the broken up bread. Boil for 10 minutes, then liquidise. (There should be visible mushroom flecks). ❹ Check the seasoning. If serving the soup immediately, reheat in a clean pan and add the cream. If preparing ahead, cool it quickly and refrigerate until needed. Do not boil once the cream has been added. Sprinkle each bowl with chopped parsley before serving.

Betty Beith
Buchanan Castle, Drymen

PINK BEETROOT AND APPLE SOUP

Serves 4

	Pinch crushed dried chillies
1	Medium onion
1	Large garlic clove
1 tbsp	Olive oil
	Knob of butter
1	Medium cooking apple
½	Small lemon
4	Medium raw beetroots, approximately 500g
1	Large potato
800ml	Hot vegetable stock

❶ Peel and finely chop or grate the onion and garlic. Heat the oil and butter in a pan and gently soften the onion and garlic. ❷ Quarter, peel and chop the apple. Toss with the juice from the half lemon. ❸ Trim and peel the potato and the beetroots, then grate on the large-hole side of a cheese grater. ❹ Add the apple and juices, crushed chillies, beetroot, potato, and a generous seasoning of salt and pepper to the softened onion. ❺ Add the hot stock and bring to the boil. Boil for 10 minutes until the apple is broken down and the beetroot and the potato are both tender. ❻ Liquidise, taste and adjust the seasoning. ❼ Serve hot with a dollop of soured cream or crème fraîche and snipped chives. Alternatively, it can be served cold and on its own.

Urmilla Lawson
Glasgow

RED CAPSICUM SOUP

Makes 1.2 litres

30g	Butter
1	Medium onion, chopped
2	Red capsicums, chopped
1	Red chilli, chopped and seeds removed
450ml	Vegetable stock
1	Large tin of chopped tomatoes
	Salt and pepper
	A few basil leaves for garnish

❶ Heat butter in frying pan. ❷ Fry onion and capsicum until onion is clear. ❸ Add chilli, stock, tomatoes, salt and pepper. ❹ Cook for 30 minutes. ❺ Blend all ingredients until smooth. ❻ Serve with basil garnish.

The soup is very easy to make and yummy to taste.

Rhona Nicol
Australia

ANNA'S SLIMMING SOUP

Serves 4

½ Cabbage, chopped
2 Celery sticks, chopped
2 Carrots, chopped
½ Turnip, chopped
1 Large onion, chopped
1 Leek, chopped
1 Red pepper, chopped
1 Medium potato, chopped
1 Courgette, chopped
1 Tin of tomatoes
  Mixed herbs
2 pts Beef stock

❶ Add all chopped ingredients to a pan with stock. ❷ Cover and simmer for 45 minutes or until all vegetables are soft. ❸ Add tomatoes and mixed herbs, bring back to the boil and serve. Delicious!

Anna MacDonald
Milngavie

SPICY LENTIL SOUP

Serves 6

	Olive or sunflower oil
100g	(4oz) Red split lentils
400g	Carrots, chopped
1	Medium onion, chopped
2	Celery sticks, chopped
1 tsp	Ground cumin
1 tsp	Ground coriander
500ml	(2 pts) Vegetable stock
400g	Tin of chopped tomatoes

❶ Heat the oil in large pan. Add onions, celery and carrots and fry gently for 3-4 minutes to soften. ❷ Add coriander and cumin and continue to cook for 3-4 minutes. ❸ Add stock, tomatoes and lentils and cook for a further 30-40 minutes, until lentils are cooked. Allow to cool for a few minutes. ❹ You can liquidise the soup now but I prefer to leave some texture so I mash it a bit with a potato masher to make it smoother but still with bits in!

I first started making this as a comforting wholesome soup when I was having chemo for breast cancer. Most lentil soup just tasted bland but the spices in this made it special. Vary amounts of cumin and coriander according to taste.

Jean Shand
Gartocharn

CURRIED SWEET POTATO AND SPINACH SOUP

Serves 4

1 tbsp	Olive oil
3	Sweet potatoes, diced
1	Onion, finely chopped
1	Garlic cloved
1½ pts	Chicken stock
1 tsp	Curry powder
½ tsp	Chilli flakes (optional)
½	Packet spinach
	Splash double cream (optional)
	Salt and pepper

❶ Heat the oil in a large saucepan and fry the onion and garlic for 5 minutes. Add the curry powder and chilli flakes (if using) and fry for 1 minute. ❷ Add the sweet potato and sweat for 5 minutes. ❸ Add the chicken stock and bring to the boil, then simmer for 20 minutes. ❹ Roughly tear the spinach and add to the pan, and simmer for a further 10 minutes. ❺ Puree the soup then return to the pan and add the cream (if using) and season well. Add some hot water if the consistency is too thick, then serve.

Fiona Maver

SWEET POTATO SOUP

Serves 2-4

1 Large sweet potato
2 Medium carrots
2 Medium potatoes
1 pt Vegetable stock
Coconut milk (optional)

❶ Peel and chop all vegetables. Add to stock and bring to the boil. Reduce heat and simmer until vegetables are soft. ❷ When cool, puree with a hand blender, then add coconut milk (optional). ❸ Best made the day before. It seems to thicken naturally.

Ellen MacKenzie
Dru Yoga Teacher

DELICIOUS PARSNIP SOUP

Serves 4-6

1½oz	Butter
1	Onion, chopped
1½lbs	Parsnips, peeled and finely diced
1 tsp	Medium curry powder
½ tsp	Ground cumin powder
2½ pts	Chicken stock
5fl oz	Fresh single cream
	Paprika to garnish
	Salt and pepper

❶ Heat butter in a large saucepan and fry onion and parsnip together until soft (5 minutes). ❷ Stir in curry powder and fry for a further 2 minutes. ❸ Add stock, bring to the boil and simmer with the lid on for 45 minutes. ❹ Season to taste. Allow to cool slightly then puree with a blender, or pass through a sieve. ❺ Return soup to pan, add cream and adjust seasoning if necessary. Heat to serving temperature, but do not boil. Serve with a sprinkling of paprika.

This recipe was given by the ex. Vicar of Witton Park, Mike and Fran (now in Darlington) and I use it very often, as it is delicious.

Dorothy Senior
Bishop Auckland

GRAN'S CREAM OF CARROT SOUP

Serves 8

2½lbs Carrots
1 Medium onion
¼lb Bacon
4 pts Stock
Double cream

❶ Peel and slice carrots. ❷ Cut bacon into small bits and sweat it with diced onion for 5 minutes. ❸ Add the sliced carrots and cook with onion and bacon for another 5 minutes. ❹ Add stock, bring to the boil and simmer for 1 hour with lid of pot slightly off. ❺ Liquidise and add cream.

This soup freezes well before you add cream.

This is a French recipe and all my grandchildren and any other visiting children just love this soup.

Sheila

EASY PEASY LEEK AND POTATO SOUP

Serves 6-8

8 Leeks, washed, trimmed and thinly sliced
4 Medium potatoes, peeled and chopped
1 tbsp Butter
1 tbsp Light olive oil
1 Fat garlic clove, chopped
3 pts Chicken stock
1 tsp Curry powder (heaped), medium or hot depending on your taste buds
Salt and pepper

❶ Heat oil and butter in a large pot. ❷ Add chopped leeks and garlic and cook for a few minutes. ❸ Add curry powder and stir well. ❹ Add potatoes and stir. ❺ Add stock and salt and pepper. ❻ Bring to the boil and simmer for 30-40 minutes, until the potatoes are soft. ❼ Use a hand blender to make a smooth and luxurious soup. ❽ Check seasoning.

Enjoy with rustic bread. Add a blob of crème fraîche and chopped chives for a smarter look. This is the easiest soup to make – so delicious to have on a cold winter's day. The heat from the curry powder is subtle and very warming.

Claire MacLellan
Garlochern

CHICKPEA AND SPINACH SOUP

Serves 2-4

1	Onion	¾ pt	Organic vegetable stock
1	Leek	2	Tins of chickpeas, rinsed and drained
1	Carrot		
1	Red pepper	1	Bag of spinach
1	Courgette		Olive oil
1	Garlic clove	2 tsp	Cumin
1	Small chilli (optional)		Salt and pepper

❶ Sauté vegetables in olive oil. ❷ Add stock and simmer for 15 minutes. ❸ Add chickpeas and spinach and stir through. ❹ Simmer for a further 10-15 minutes, then liquidise, season and enjoy.

Serve with crusty bread!

Lee Beveridge
Bearsden

CAULIFLOWER AND POTATO SOUP

Serves 4-6

1 Medium cauliflower
1 Medium potato
(don't overdo the potato)
1½ litre Stock (you can use a
stock cube)
2 Leeks, trimmed
1 tbsp Butter or olive oil
40g Grated Parmesan
(about a handful)
Grated nutmeg
Salt and pepper

❶ Cut the cauliflower into small florets. Peel and dice the potato. Bring the stock to the boil, and then add the salt, potato and cauliflower. ❷ Cook for 15 minutes. ❸ Trim the leeks and slice them thinly. Melt the butter in a pan and cook the leeks slowly until soft. ❹ Add the leeks to the cauliflower and potato mixture and simmer together for 5 minutes. ❺ Purée the soup in a blender and return to the pan. Simmer gently for a further 5 minutes. ❻ Add the Parmesan and nutmeg, stirring gently. Season and serve.

Jennifer Murray
Madrid

JULIE'S LENTIL SOUP

Serves 4-6

2 litres	Water
3-4	Ham stock cubes
3-5	Bacon bits/rashers
½	Packet of lentils
4-5	Carrots
1	Leek
1-2	Medium potatoes
4-5	Garlic cloves
1	Tin of butter beans (optional)

❶ Boil the water and add the stock cubes. ❷ Add the chopped carrots, leeks, potatoes and lentils and leave to boil. ❸ Fry the bacon and add to the soup. ❹ Lower the heat once boiling and add the garlic. ❺ Add the butter beans if you want (I never do). ❻ Leave to cook for 30 minutes. ❼ Pick out the garlic and blend – and your soup is ready!

Delicious, yummy lentil soup – the garlic cloves add a nice flavour. If you like thick soup, go for extra lentils, and the butter beans. Adjust the quantities to find a flavour that matches your taste. This is exactly how I like my lentil soup.

Julie Fraser
Dollar

SPICY BUTTERNUT SQUASH SOUP

Serves 2-4

1	Medium onion, chopped
2 tbsp	Olive oil
1	Medium butternut squash, cubed
500ml	Vegetable stock
1 tsp	Mild curry paste (or ½ dsp curry powder)
	Coriander
	Salt and pepper

❶ Heat oil in pan and add the onion and butternut squash. Cook for 5 minutes. ❷ Add the vegetable stock and curry paste/powder. ❸ Add a little coriander, salt and pepper. ❹ Cover and simmer for 30 minutes. ❺ Allow to cool. ❻ Blend with hand blender or liquidiser. ❼ Reheat and serve.

Gladys Cadden
Buchanan Castle, Drymen

COCK-A-LEEKIE SOUP

Serves 4-6

Knob butter
4 Chicken thighs, cut into small chunks
1 Leek, finely chopped
2 Chicken stock cubes
1 cup Long grain rice (basmati)

❶ Melt butter and add white part of leek and cook until soft. ❷ Add chicken and cook for further 10 minutes. ❸ Add boiled water to cover and crumble in 2 stock cubes and green part of leeks. ❹ Skim any fat that rises to the surface. Cook for 20 minutes, then add rice and simmer for a further 20 minutes.

This soup is Scottish comfort food at its best. When it's cold and dreich outside, this will definitely warm you up!

Janey Mckay
Killearn

GAMBA FISH SOUP WITH CRAB MEAT, STEM GINGER AND CORIANDER

275g	White fish meat (haddock, cod or whiting)
4	Garlic cloves
50g	Root ginger
2	Medium onions, chopped
50g	Unsalted butter
3 tbsp	Plain flour
1.15 litre	Fish stock
1	Packet of coriander
50g	Stem ginger, grated
3 tbsp	Tomato purée
450g	White crab meat
75ml	Brandy

❶ Melt the butter over a low heat in a thick-bottomed pan. ❷ Chop the onions, garlic and root ginger and sweat in a covered pan with the butter. Add brandy and reduce. ❸ Mix in the flour and cook out for about 5 minutes, still on a low heat. Add the tomato purée and keep mixing. Start adding the fish stock little by little, mixing all the time. ❹ Add the white fish meat and cook for about 30-40 minutes. ❺ Liquidise the soup and pass through a sieve into a clean pot or bowl. Add the crabmeat, grated stem ginger and chopped coriander. ❻ Serve in warm bowls with garlic bread.

Derek A Marshall
Head Chef, Gamba Restaurant and Bar, Glasgow

SINA'S MIXED BEAN AND BACON SOUP

Serves 4-6

2 tbsp	Olive oil
1	Onion, thinly sliced
6oz	Smoked bacon, diced
2	Garlic cloves, crushed
1	Celery, sliced
2	Carrots, diced
1	Tin of tomatoes
1	Tin of mixed beans, drained
1 tsp	Dried oregano
1½ pts	Vegetable stock

❶ Sauté the onion, bacon and garlic together until the onion is soft. ❷ Add the remaining fresh vegetables. ❸ Then add the liquid from the tinned tomatoes to the mixture, followed by the vegetable stock and the tomatoes. ❹ Simmer for 15 minutes. ❺ Add the drained beans. ❻ Cook for 3-4 minutes.

Serve with crusty bread.

Sina Stewart
Bearsden

POULTRY

15 MINUTE SUNNY CHICKEN PASTA

Serves 4

2 Chicken breast fillets
1 Jar of sun-dried tomatoes
1 Large tub of half fat
crème fraîche
1 Garlic clove, crushed
Dried oregano
Dried basil
1 Small packet of pasta
(shells/bows/penne
works best)

❶ Pour a small amount of oil from the sun-dried tomatoes into a large frying pan/ wok and heat gently. ❷ Add garlic, oregano and basil, together with chicken breasts (chopped into small pieces). Stir until chicken is cooked. ❸ Drain the oil and thinly slice the sun-dried tomatoes. ❹ Cook and then drain the pasta (follow instructions on packet ie if fresh will only take 4 minutes). ❺ Add the sun-dried tomatoes into the pan with chicken – stir for 2-3 minutes. ❻ Mix the chicken and the cooked pasta together. ❼ Lastly stir crème fraîche into the chicken and pasta mixture. Pour into large serving bowl and serve immediately. Serve with mixed salad and warm garlic bread.

This was a dish that my cousin in Los Angeles made for me when I visited her and it tastes really good and only takes 15 minutes!!!

Elaine Sherlock
Balloch

MANGO CHICKEN

Serves 4

- 4 Chicken breasts
- 1 Jar mango chutney
- 1 tsp Curry powder
  (strength to taste)
  Knob of butter or
  low fat spread
  Water

① Cut each chicken breast lengthwise into 3. Arrange in casserole dish.
② Mix chutney, curry powder, butter and about half a jar of water and pour over chicken. ③ Cover and bake for 40 minutes at 180°C.

Serve with boiled potatoes or rice and green vegetables.

Sally Windebank
Milngavie

CHICKEN AND BLACK PUDDING STOVIES

Serves 4

2	Chicken breasts, diced
4	Slices black pudding
1	Onion, sliced
1	Large jar creamy peppercorn sauce
500g	King Edward potatoes, thinly sliced
200ml	Double cream
100ml	Milk
1	Garlic clove, crushed
50g	Gruyere cheese, grated

Preheat the oven to 180°C/Gas Mark 4 and place the sliced potatoes in a bowl of cold water to prevent them from browning. Rinse then pat dry with kitchen roll. ❶ Place the cream, milk and garlic in a large saucepan and bring to a gentle simmer. ❷ Add the potatoes, season well, cover and simmer for about 5 minutes, stirring occasionally. ❸ In another saucepan gently fry the black pudding in a little olive oil, then remove to a plate. ❹ Fry the chicken for a few minutes, then add the onion and fry until soft. ❺ Add the peppercorn sauce and heat through. ❻ Roughly chop the black pudding and add to the chicken mixture. Add a little extra cream if the mixture is too thick. ❼ Transfer the chicken and black pudding mixture to a buttered ovenproof dish, then spread the potatoes on top. Sprinkle the cheese on top. ❽ Bake for 25 minutes and serve with vegetables of your choice.

A friend at work tried this at a restaurant in Glasgow and I thought it sounded wonderful so I made this recipe up from her description. It's really easy to make and is absolutely delicious. It would also work well with haggis.

Fiona Maver

THAI RED CHICKEN CURRY

Serves 4

1 tbsp	Vegetable oil
800ml	Coconut milk (2 tins)
4 tbsp	Thai red curry paste
450g	Chicken thighs, skinless and sliced into strips
110g	Tin of bamboo shoots, drained
2	Red peppers, thinly sliced
2 tbsp	Thai fish sauce
1 tsp	Sugar
2 tbsp	Basil or coriander leaves, chopped
2	Red chillies, sliced diagonally (optional)
4	Kaffir lime leaves (optional)

❶ Heat oil on moderate heat in a large heavy based saucepan and add red curry paste. Fry for a few seconds and add 400ml tin coconut milk. Heat until the milk becomes fragrant, stirring occasionally. ❷ Add chicken and simmer, stirring frequently, until it changes colour. ❸ Add second tin of coconut milk, red pepper, kaffir lime leaves (if using) and bamboo shoots. Bring to boil, reduce the heat to low and simmer uncovered until chicken is tender. ❹ Stir in fish sauce, sugar and basil or coriander and simmer for 5 minutes. Garnish with sliced chillies, if using. Serve with rice.

Joe Musgrave
Buchanan Castle, Drymen

CHILLI CHICKEN

Serves 4

2 tbsp	Vegetable or groundnut oil
450g	Chicken breast or thigh, cut into small pieces
1-2	Green or red chillies
1	Green pepper, sliced lengthways
1	Large onion, sliced lengthways
2	Garlic cloves, crushed
2 tbsp	Cornflour
3 tbsp	Light soy sauce

❶ Marinate the chicken with soy sauce and chopped chillies for half an hour.
❷ Heat 1 tablespoon of the oil in a wok or large pan, lift chicken from marinade, reserving the marinade and stir-fry the chicken for a few minutes. Set aside.
❸ Mix cornflour in a little cold water and set aside. ❹ Heat remaining oil in a pan and put in the crushed garlic. Stir-fry for 1 minute and add the onion and green pepper, chilli and soy sauce. ❺ Stir-fry for another minute and add the chicken. Stir-fry for a couple of minutes and add the cornflour and water mixture. Cook until the chicken is properly coated and hot. Serve with rice or noodles.

Ujani Andrews
Calcutta, India

CHICKEN DIVAN

Serves 4

Broccoli or cauliflower for
covering bottom of dish
Chopped chicken (cooked)
2 Tins of condensed soup of
your choice
Mayonnaise (add to taste)
1 tsp Curry powder
1 tsp Lemon juice
Grated cheese to cover top
Crisps, crushed (to cover
top of cheese)

❶ Arrange half cooked broccoli or cauliflower in greased dish. ❷ Place cooked chicken on top. ❸ Combine soup, mayonnaise, curry powder and lemon juice and pour over chicken. ❹ Top with grated cheese and then with the crisps. Dot with butter. ❺ Cook for 45 minutes at 190°C/Gas Mark 5.

Janice King

EASY CHICKEN LAKSA

Serves 4

400g	Chicken, diced		1 tbsp	Dried coriander
2 tbsp	Olive oil		1 tsp	Lemongrass
2 tsp	Garlic, crushed		1 tsp	Turmeric
2 tsp	Ginger, crushed		500ml	Chicken stock
3 tsp	Curry paste		125g	Soft noodles
1	Carrot, diced		1 tbsp	Cornflour
2	Peppers, diced		1 tsp	Coconut essence
2 cups	Shallots, diced		300ml	Evaporated light milk

❶ In a large frying pan add the oil and sauté the chicken, garlic, curry paste and ginger together. ❷ Add the carrots and peppers and cook for a further 2 minutes. ❸ Place shallots, coriander, lemongrass, turmeric, chicken stock and noodles in the pan and combine well. ❹ Mix coconut essence, cornflour and evaporated milk together, then mix with the other ingredients. ❺ Simmer for 10 minutes and serve garnished with coriander.

Note: Prawns can be substituted for the chicken and celery for the peppers.

This recipe is really simple, but can be personalised by making the curry paste from scratch or by adding monkfish or red snapper and more vegetables to the dish.

Fiona Fox
Buchanan Castle, Drymen

CHICKEN WITH MUSTARD AND CREAM SAUCE

Serves 4

4	Chicken portions		4	Shallots, finely chopped
2 tbsp	Plain flour		1	Bouquet garni
	Salt and pepper		¼ pt	Dry white wine
2 tbsp	Olive oil		¼ pt	Chicken stock
2 tbsp	Butter		1 tsp	English mustard
4oz	Streaky bacon, diced and blanched		1 tsp	French mustard
			½ pt	Double cream

❶ Roll chicken in flour, season and cook with bacon in oil and butter until golden. ❷ Add shallots, bouquet garni, wine and stock and cover with lid and cook gently until tender. ❸ Drain chicken pieces and place in a heated casserole dish. Keep hot. Skim fat from sauce. ❹ Whisk mustards and cream thoroughly, being careful not to over whisk, and add to sauce in pan. ❺ Adjust seasoning if necessary, add chicken pieces and heat through. Transfer chicken and sauce back to casserole dish and serve. Serve with either rice or new potatoes and vegetables or salad.

Christine Gastall
Drymen

CASSEROLE OF LOCAL PHEASANT

Serves 2

1	Pheasant, jointed
200g	Mushrooms
1 tbsp	Flour
½ pt	Stock
¼ pt	Orange juice
¼ pt	White wine

❶ Brown pheasant in oil. ❷ Brown mushrooms in a separate pan and then add to pheasant. ❸ Stir flour in to the juices in pan and cook. ❹ Add stock, orange juice and white wine then boil and add to casserole. ❺ Cook at Gas Mark 4 for 1 hour. ❻ Garnish with orange peel and segments.

Hannah Taylor

CHICKEN AND HAM PIE

Serves 6

8 oz	**Cooked chicken**
4-6 oz	**Cooked ham**
	Pineapple chunks (tinned)
	Philadelphia cream cheese
	Puff pastry (ready-rolled)

❶ Mix together cream cheese, chicken, ham, and as many pineapple chunks as you want. ❷ Lay rolled pastry on a flat surface, place mixture down the centre, and then fold sides up to seal. ❸ Turn over onto baking tray, so that the join is underneath. Score the pastry and brush with egg or milk. ❹ Cook in an oven at 175°C until pastry is cooked.

Wilma Snoddy

BAKED CHICKEN WITH PARMESAN AND WHOLEGRAIN MUSTARD

Serves 4

4	Chicken breasts, skinned and diced
60g	Parmesan cheese, freshly grated
1 tbsp	Wholegrain mustard
225 ml	Double cream
150 ml	Chicken stock
2 tsp	Cornflour dissolved in cold water

❶ Place the diced chicken in an ovenproof dish, cover with the cheese and mustard and mix well. ❷ Combine the cream, stock and cornflour then pour over the chicken. ❸ Season with freshly ground black pepper and bake uncovered in an oven preheated to 170°C/325°F/Gas Mark 3 for 35 minutes.

Hazel Mills
Belfast

ROSEMARY AND PEPPER CHICKEN

Serves 4

1	Red pepper
	Salt and pepper
1	Yellow pepper
14oz	Tin of chopped tomatoes
1 tbsp	Olive oil
4	Chicken leg joints halved
2 tbsp	Olive oil
2 tbsp	Rosemary, chopped
1 tsp	Dried oregano
	Lemon wedges and fresh rosemary to garnish

❶ Core and deseed peppers and chop into large pieces. ❷ Mix with oil in roasting tin and bake for 20 minutes until slightly roasted. ❸ Remove from oven and stir in tomatoes, oregano, and seasoning. Bake for further 10 minutes. ❹ Season chicken. Heat oil in frying pan, fry chicken for 5 minutes until browned. ❺ Add chopped rosemary and reduce the heat. ❻ Cover pan and cook for a further 35 minutes until chicken is tender. ❼ Pour pepper and tomato mixture over the chicken and bring to the boil. Serve and garnish with lemon wedges and sprig of fresh rosemary. Good with croquettes and courgettes.

Felicity Molyneux

CHICKEN WITH APPLES AND CIDER

Serves 4

2 tbsp	Oil
4	Chicken breasts, skinless and boneless
1	Onion, cut into wedges
2	Eating apples, peeled, cored and cut into 8 wedges each
500ml	Dry cider
150ml	Chicken stock
	Rice or mash to serve

❶ Heat oil in a large frying pan and fry chicken breasts for 3-4 minutes each side until golden. Remove from pan and set aside. ❷ Lower heat and add onion, fry for 2-3 minutes until tinged brown. ❸ Add the apple and cook over heat for 5 minutes until golden. ❹ Still on a high heat, pour in cider and bubble for 2 minutes to reduce slightly. ❺ Add the stock, stirring to scrape the 'bits' from the bottom of the pan. ❻ Lower heat and return chicken to pan, cover and simmer for 5 minutes until almost cooked. ❼ Remove lid and simmer for 3-4 minutes to thicken sauce a little. Serve with rice or mash.

Works well with pork steaks too.

Felicity Molyneux

CHICKEN AND LEEK POT PIES

Serves 4

500g	Parsnips, chopped
300g	Floury potatoes, chopped
4	Leeks, sliced
1	Lemon, zested
500g	Chicken breasts, skinless and boneless, chopped
2 tbsp	Parsley, chopped
2 tsp	Cornflour
2 tbsp	Low fat crème fraîche
1 tbsp	Olive oil
1 tbsp	Wholegrain mustard

Preheat oven to 200°C/Fan 180°C/Gas Mark 6. ❶ Boil parsnips and potatoes until tender, drain reserving the water then mash with a little seasoning. ❷ Toss chicken in the cornflour. ❸ Heat oil in a large pan, add the leeks then fry for 3 minutes until starting to soften. ❹ Add the chicken and 200ml of water from the potatoes, and bring to the boil stirring. ❺ Reduce heat, and gently simmer for 10 minutes, until chicken is just tender. ❻ Remove from the heat, and stir in lemon zest, parsley, crème fraîche and mustard. ❼ Divide the chicken filling between 4 x 300ml pie dishes, spoon over the mash and spread roughly with a fork to seal the filling. ❽ Bake for 25 minutes until the topping is crisp and golden.

Good source of folic acid and vitamin C. You can make a big pie if you prefer using a 1-2 litre pie dish and increase the cooking time by 10 minutes.

Trisha Davie
Glasgow

CHILLI CHICKEN WITH CHORIZO

Serves 6-8

6-8	Chicken breasts	1 tsp	Dried chilli flakes
	Olive oil	1 tsp	Ground cumin
	Garlic	2 tsps	Oregano
1	Chorizo ring (or similar)	2 tsps	Cumin seeds
2	Onions	1-2	Tins of kidney beans
3	Red peppers	1	Tin of cannellini beans
2	Tins of tomatoes		
2	Chicken stock cubes		

I cook on the stove first in a big shallow pot with lid. ❶ Fry chicken, onion, garlic for about 5 minutes – add all spices and cook for a further 5 minutes. ❷ Add tomatoes and chicken stock cubes and cook for a further 10 minutes. ❸ Then add peppers (I leave them in biggish chunks), beans and chorizo then cook for about a further 10-15 minutes. You can either cook through to finish but I usually have done all this the night before or earlier in the day and then I put whole pot in the oven about 170°C for about 25 minutes before serving. Just keep tasting it – and it's even better reheated the next day. I serve with rice, salad, sour cream and guacamole.

Caroline Clark
Drymen

CHICKEN PASSANDA

Serves 2

3	Chicken breasts, cubed
1	Tin of evaporated milk
4oz	Ground almonds
2 tbsp	Flaked almonds
4oz	Plain yoghurt
4oz	Double cream
2 tbsp	Tomato puree
3 tbsp	Mango chutney
1	Onion, finely chopped
2 tsp	Curry powder
½ tsp	Chilli powder

1	Cayenne chilli (optional), finely chopped
4	Garlic cloves, crushed
2"	Root ginger, grated
5 tbsp	Vegetable oil
4 tbsp	Coriander leaves, roughly chopped
1 tbsp	Whole coriander leaves
1 tsp	Turmeric
1 tsp	Garam masala

❶ Make a paste with the curry powder, turmeric and chilli powder and a little water. ❷ Stir fry on a medium heat until translucent in the vegetable oil then add the garlic, ginger and chillies and stir fry on a medium heat for a further 5 minutes. ❸ Add the curry and chilli powder paste and stir in and fry for a further 30 seconds. ❹ Add the chicken pieces and seal well on all sides. ❺ Stir in the cream, tomato puree, ground almonds, mango chutney and milk and simmer for 20 minutes or until the chicken is cooked, stirring constantly. If needed add a little water to prevent the curry becoming too thick or dry. ❻ Now stir in the garam masala and finely chopped coriander leaves and cook for a further minute. Serve with the whole coriander leaves sprinkled over the top.

John Hair
Glasgow

PUNJABI STYLE CHICKEN CURRY

Serves 4-6

1	Large onion	1 tsp	Fenugreek (dried leaf if possible)
1	Block Lurpak butter		Bunch of coriander (must be fresh)
1"	Ginger, very finely chopped		
4	Garlic cloves, very finely chopped	8-12	Medium green chillies, very finely chopped
½ tsp	Salt	½-1	Tin of peeled plum tomatoes
1 tsp	Black peppercorns, crushed		
2 tsp	Fennel seed	1	Red or green pepper (optional)
4 tsp	Cumin seed		
2 tsp	Paprika	2lb	Chicken (or lamb, beef, etc)
2 tsp	Turmeric		
3 tsps	Garam masala		

❶ Melt butter in large pan over low heat. Add finely sliced onion and cook for about 20-25 minutes stirring often. ❷ Add garlic and ginger. Stir continuously for 5 minutes. ❸ Grind pepper, fennel and cumin (in small coffee grinder or pestle and mortar), mix in turmeric, paprika and salt thoroughly and add to pan. Stir vigorously and add meat and chillies. ❹ Stir continuously over a high heat until meat changes colour. ❺ Reduce heat to low and continue stirring for 5 minutes – there should now be plenty of juice. Cook for 20 minutes stirring often then add tomatoes and 1-1½ cups cold water. Simmer for 40 minutes. ❻ Take leaves from stalks of coriander. Wash leaves and add along with garam masala and fenugreek, green/red pepper (optional) to pan. Cook for 5-10 minutes. Serve with basmati rice and enjoy.

Sam Fairhurst/M.Hanif
Irvine/India

INDONESIAN MARINATED CHICKEN

Serves 8

Marinade:		Potatoes:	
1	Onion, quartered	3	Sweet potatoes
1"	Fresh ginger	1	Red onion
2 tbsp	Runny honey	2	Red peppers
6 tbsp	Light soy sauce	2	Garlic cloves, crushed
2 tbsp	Sambal olek (hot chilli paste will do)	1 tbsp	Balsamic vinegar
			Salt and pepper
2	Limes, juiced		
8	Chicken thighs		

❶ Preheat the oven to 200°C/400°F/Gas Mark 6. ❷ Marinade: Whizz all ingredients in a food processor and pulse to a coarse paste, spread over the chicken coating well. This can be done the day before, keep covered and bring to room temperature before cooking. ❸ Potatoes: cut the potatoes, onions, peppers into similar sized chunks. Place in a baking dish with the garlic, oil and vinegar, season and toss the vegetables so they are really well covered. ❹ Roast until tender and slightly caramelised, about 40 minutes. ❺ Heat a cast iron griddle until very hot and sear the chicken (take out of marinade) on all sides until well covered. ❻ Transfer to a roasting tin, pour over the marinade and roast until cooked through for about 30 minutes. Serve with Greek style yoghurt with some fresh coriander.

Sambal olek can be bought from Chinese and Asian shops.

Becky Walker
Buchlyvie

CHICKEN FRIED RICE WITH BASIL

Serves 4-6

14fl oz	Thai jasmine rice, long grain white rice or basmati rice
8oz	Chicken breasts, boneless and skinless
2 tbsp	Vegetable oil
3 tbsp	Garlic, finely sliced
1	Small onion, finely chopped
3 tbsp	Shallots, finely sliced
3 tbsp	Spring onion, finely shredded

5	Large fresh chillies, seeded and finely chopped (use 2-3 if you want it milder)
2 tsp	Sugar
1 tbsp	Fish sauce
	Salt and pepper
	Large handful of fresh basil leaves, shredded

❶ At least 2 hours before (or the night before) cook the rice according to instructions on packet. ❷ Spread rice out on a baking tray to allow it to cool thoroughly and put it in the fridge. ❸ Cut the chicken into thin strips then set aside. ❹ Place a large wok or frying pan over a high heat and add the oil. Once the oil has heated add the garlic, onion, shallots, chillies, salt and pepper then stir fry for 2 minutes. ❺ Add chicken and stir fry for 3 minutes. ❻ Add cold rice and continue to stir fry for 3 minutes. ❼ Add sugar and fish sauce and stir fry for 2 minutes. ❽ Take off the heat and add the basil stirring through. Serve in a large bowl and scatter the spring onions over to garnish.

This can be eaten hot or left to cool and served as a rice salad.

Jacqui Crawford
Glasgow

BAKED CHICKEN WITH CHUTNEY AND MUSTARD

Serves 6

6 tbsp **Chutney (eg mango)**
3 tbsp **Mustard**
2 tbsp **Oil**
6 **Chicken breasts**

❶ Mix chutney, mustard and oil together and smear mixture over chicken in an ovenproof dish. Do this several hours in advance and keep dish covered in a fridge. ❷ An hour before cooking, take dish out of fridge and leave at room temperature. ❸ Bake in a hot oven 200°C/400°F/Gas Mark 6 for 25 minutes – pierce chicken breast to check that juices which run are clear to see if it is cooked through. This cooking time is right for average size chicken breasts. If mixture is getting too brown put a piece of greaseproof paper over the top. Serve with green vegetables (broccoli, stir fried cabbage) and mashed potatoes or rice.

This is very easy and appeals to children and adults

Fiona Dewar
Gartocharn

CHICKEN MOZZARELLA

Serves 6

6 Chicken breasts
12 Slices mozzarella cheese
12 Slices of bacon
Fresh basil leaves
Garlic, crushed
1 Large tin of chopped tomatoes
Glass of dry white wine

❶ Slice open the chicken breasts into butterflies. ❷ Place 2 slices of mozzarella and 2-3 basil leaves on one side of each breast. ❸ Fold each chicken breast and wrap in 2 slices of bacon. ❹ Arrange the wrapped parcels in an oven proof dish. ❺ Mix together the chopped tomatoes, crushed garlic and wine. Pour over the chicken parcels. ❻ Cover dish with tinfoil and cook in moderate oven until chicken is cooked through (about 30-40 minutes). Serve with boiled rice.

Jacqui Crawford
Glasgow

JENNY'S CREAMY TARRAGON CHICKEN

Serves 6

- 1 Medium/large chicken
- 2 Onions, chopped
- 1 Clove garlic, chopped
- ½ Tin of chopped tomatoes
- 2 Chicken stock cubes
  Pepper
  Tarragon
- 2 Small tubs low fat
  crème fraîche
  Handful of flaked almonds
  Buttered breadcrumbs or
  crisps to cover

Preheat oven to 180°C. ❶ Joint chicken. Remove all excess skin and fat.
❷ Brown chicken then transfer to a large shallow baking dish, no lid needed.
❸ Fry chopped onions and garlic in oil and add more if needed to soften.
❹ Then add chopped tomatoes, stock cubes, herbs and simmer for 5 minutes.
❺ Add almonds, then enough crème fraîche to make mixture pink and check
seasoning. ❻ Pour mixture over chicken pieces and cover with buttered
breadcrumbs. Cook in oven for 45 minutes or until chicken is tender.

Jenny O'Keefe
Croftamie

CHICKEN MYERS

Serves 4-6

2 tbsp	**Fresh double cream**
4-6	**Chicken pieces**
10½fl oz	**Tin of Campbell's condensed cream of chicken soup**
½ tsp	**Curry powder (level)**
2 tbsp	**Real mayonnaise (rounded)**
2oz	**Cheddar cheese**

❶ Roll chicken in seasoned flour and place in a baking dish. ❷ Combine soup, mayonnaise, cream and curry powder and spoon over chicken. ❸ Cover with grated cheese. ❹ Bake at 375°F for about 45 minutes uncovered.

Hope you will like this!

This lady, Christine Carson, died about a year ago but I know she would have wanted me to pass this on. She survived cancer for 20 years.

Val MacDonald
Dyrnan

CHICKEN CASSEROLE

Serves 4-6

1	Chicken (cut up) or chicken breasts
2 tbsp	Vinegar
¼ cup	Tomato sauce
1 tbsp	Brown sauce
2 tbsp	Brown sugar
1 tsp	Mustard (dry)
2 tbsp	Butter
	Salt and pepper

❶ Put all ingredients in pot, except chicken, and bring to the boil, on cooker.
❷ Pour sauce over chicken, cook 1-2 hours at Gas Mark 6. Serve with rice and salad. It's easy and tasty!

It does taste delicious, passed down from my mum's mum in South Africa and I use it often.

Bev Reid
Buchanan Castle, Drymen

CHICKEN MARINATED IN A SPICY SAUCE

Serves 2

4	Chicken thighs, boned and skinned
½ tsp	Fresh ginger, thinly sliced
½ tsp	Red chilli, finely sliced
1	Shallot, peeled and sliced
2	Garlic cloves, finely sliced
1 tbsp	Brown sugar
1 tbsp	Honey
4 tbsp	Light soy sauce
4 tbsp	Rice wine or vinegar
1 tbsp	Olive oil
1 tbsp	Tomato sauce

❶ Make up sauce, combining all the above ingredients. ❷ Put prepared chicken pieces in a bowl and stir in sauce, making sure the chicken is well covered. Cover with cling film, and leave to marinate for 1½-2 hrs, spooning sauce over chicken once or twice during that time. ❸ Heat the oven to 180°C. ❹ Transfer prepared chicken to a heatproof dish, cover with foil and cook for 40-45 minutes, taking foil off for the last 10 minutes and stirring mixture at the same time. Serve with boiled rice mixed with pineapple pieces, sliced spring onions, sweet chilli peppers and a green salad.

Sybil and Dereck Fowles
Buchanan Castle, Drymen

SUMMER WARM CHICKEN SALAD

Serves 6

3 Cooked chicken breasts, diced
1 Pack of grilled bacon, diced
12 Boiled new potatoes either sliced thickly or quartered
1 Small bottle (175ml) French dressing, or make your own

1 Pack of mixed salad leaves
175ml Single cream
1 Large handful of Parmesan cheese (more can be added for individuals taste)
Salt and pepper

❶ Heat the French dressing in a pan, add the Parmesan, after a few minutes add the cream. ❷ Continue stirring and add the chicken, bacon and potatoes. Once all the ingredients are in, warm through. It is now ready to serve.

I like to put the salad in a large bowl and then pour everything on top, sprinkle with some grated Parmesan to finish. Serve immediately. Everyone helps themselves, I also have warm bread eg focaccia or French bread ready to be served at the same time. The bread is good for dunking in any left over sauce in the bowl. If you like you can add to the salad eg chopped spring onions, chopped tomatoes, cucumber etc, these are all optional.

Also, a nice glass of crisp dry white wine goes down very nicely with lots of chat from your friends.

Hope you like this!

Mairi McGinn
Balmaha

MURIEL'S CHICKEN MYERS

Serves 4-6

4-6	Chicken pieces
10½fl oz	Condensed chicken soup
4 tbsp	Mayonnaise
4 tbsp	Double cream
½ tsp	Curry powder (level)
4 oz	Cheddar cheese, grated

❶ Mix all the ingredients together. ❷ Cook in the oven at Gas Mark 5 for 30 minutes.

Muriel Findlay
Bearsden

BAKED CHICKEN WITH PARMESAN

Serves 4

- 4 **Chicken breasts, skinned and diced**
- 60g **Parmesan cheese, freshly grated**
- 1 tbsp **Wholegrain mustard**
- 225ml **Double cream**
- 150ml **Chicken stock**
- 2 tsp **Cornflour dissolved in cold water**

① Place the diced chicken in an ovenproof dish and cover with the cheese and mustard and mix well. ② Combine the cream, stock and cornflour then pour over the chicken. ③ Season with fresly ground black pepper and bake uncovered in preheated oven at 175°C/325°F/Gas Mark 3 for 35 minutes. Enjoy!

Hazel Mills

MEAT

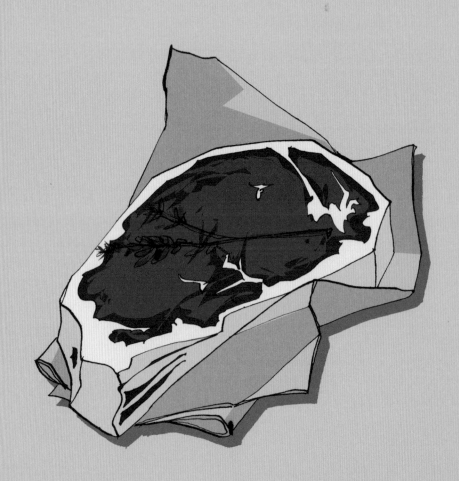

LAMB STIR FRY

Serves 4

½lb	Lamb fillet, thinly sliced	1	Red pepper
8	Lamb kidneys, quartered	1	Red chilli
1 tsp	Ginger	8	Basil leaves
1	Garlic clove	8	Mint leaves
6oz	White button mushrooms, quartered	½ tsp	Tabasco sauce
1 tbsp	Sesame seed oil	1 tbsp	Soy sauce
	Bunch spring onions		

❶ Marinate lamb and kidneys in the tabasco and soy sauce. ❷ Heat oil, add strips of garlic and ginger. Add red pepper cut in thick strips, chopped red chilli and 1 inch pieces of spring onion. ❸ Add lamb and kidneys to vegetables and reserve marinade. ❹ Toss and season. ❺ Add mushrooms, strips of basil and mint. ❻ Add marinade, check seasoning and serve on rice or cous cous.

This is a favourite quick stir fry which I have used since time began!

Pat Rushton,
Dartmouth

CASSEROLED LAMB WITH TOMATO AND PESTO

Serves 6-8

1.5kg	(1lb) Lamb, cut roughly into 1"/2½cm chunks and trimmed of excessive fat
2 tbsp	Flour
	Salt and pepper
3 tbsp	Olive oil
2	Medium onions, skinned and finely sliced
2	Garlic cloves, skinned and finely chopped
2 x 400g	(15oz) Tins of tomatoes
½ pt	(300ml) Dry white wine
	Pinch of sugar
2 tbsp	Pesto

❶ Season the flour with salt and pepper. Coat the pieces of lamb with the flour. ❷ Heat the olive oil in a heavy casserole, and brown the pieces of lamb all over, a few at a time. Keep the browned lamb warm in a low oven. ❸ Add the onions to the oil and meat juices in the casserole and sauté for about 5 minutes, until they are transparent. ❹ Then add the garlic and the tomatoes, breaking the tomatoes up against the sides of the casserole with your wooden spoon. ❺ Stir in the white wine, sugar and pesto, season and bring to the boil. ❻ Return the browned lamb to the casserole, cover with a lid, and cook for 1 hour in a moderate oven – 180°C/Gas Mark 4/bottom right oven in 4 door Aga.

Like so many casseroles, this one tastes even better if made a day in advance. This is one of my favourite lamb recipes. It is easy to make and the family love it.

Sheila Harvie
Mugdock

LAMB DOPIAZA

Serves 6-8

2-3 tbsp	Vegetable oil		½-1 tsp	Chilli powder
1 kg	Lamb shoulder or leg, boned and cubed		2 tsp	Cumin powder
6	Medium potatoes, peeled and cut into medium pieces		2 tsp	Coriander powder
			1 tsp	Turmeric
2	Large onions, thinly sliced		3	Tomatoes, chopped
3	Garlic cloves, chopped finely		6 tbsp	Natural yoghurt
2"	Piece ginger, peeled and chopped			Salt and pepper
				Fresh coriander, chopped

❶ Heat oil in large heavy-based pan. Brown the onions on a medium heat remove with slotted spoon. ❷ Turn up heat, add lamb and brown in stages, adding a little more oil if needed to prevent the meat sticking. ❸ Place onions back in pan with the meat and add garlic. Stir for 2 minutes. ❹ Add chilli, cumin, coriander and turmeric powder and stir for a further 2 minutes. ❺ Make ginger into a paste with a little water in a blender or with a pestle and mortar and add to lamb. ❻ Add chopped tomatoes. Simmer for a few minutes. ❼ Add yoghurt 1 tablespoon at a time, stirring each spoonful into the lamb. Bring to the boil and simmer for 5 minutes. ❽ Add potatoes, bring the lamb and potatoes to a simmer place a lid on the pan. Add salt and pepper to taste and simmer for approximately 30 minutes until lamb is tender and potatoes are cooked. Sprinkle with chopped coriander to serve.

This is a favourite for special occasions but is really easy and tastes great any time!

Sharmi Musgrave
Buchanan Castle, Drymen

ARABIAN LAMB

Serves 6-8

3 tbsp	Oil	¾ pt	Lamb or beef stock
3	Onions, sliced		Seasoning
2	Garlic cloves, crushed	10	Button onions
3	Cloves	4	Small carrots
1	Bay leaf	2	Medium potatoes
1¼lbs	Boneless lamb, cubed	7oz	Easy cook rice
4 tbsp	Tomato puree	3oz	Vermicelli
1½ tbsp	Arabic spice (see note)		

❶ Fry sliced onions, garlic and bay leaf in a deep pan until brown. Push contents to 1 side or remove. ❷ Brown lamb. ❸ Add the tomato puree and Arabic spices and cook for 1 minute. ❹ Stir in stock, season and simmer covered for 45-50 minutes. ❺ Meanwhile, peel button onions, cut carrots into short lengths. ❻ Cut peeled potatoes in even sized quarter pieces. ❼ Add the vegetables and cook for a further 25 minutes. ❽ Have the hot rice and vermicelli (boiled separately) ready. ❾ Toss them together in a dish and top with the lamb and vegetable mixture.

Note: Arabic Spice. If you cannot get Arabic Spices – mix ½ a teaspoon of the following together: Crushed black pepper, ground coriander, cassia, cloves, cumin, cardamom, nutmeg and paprika. Any left over can be kept in a jar for the next time.

Hannah Taylor

SRI LANKAN LAMB CURRY

Serves 4

2 tsp	Whole mustard seeds	3	Whole cardamom pods
¼ tsp	Whole peppercorns	30g	Fresh coriander, chopped
3 tbsp	Whole coriander seeds	12	Curry leaves
1½ tsp	Red chilli powder	450g	Stewing lean lamb, cubed
60g	Shallots, chopped		(you may use beef or pork)
1cm	Piece of fresh ginger, peeled and chopped	350ml	Coconut milk (shaken well)
		¾ tsp	Maldon salt to taste
3	Medium garlic cloves, peeled and chopped	3 tbsp	Corn oil

❶ Put mustard seeds, peppercorns and coriander seeds into a clean spice/coffee grinder. Grind as finely as possible. Heat pan and pour in the oil. ❷ Fry oil until opaque. Add in the garlic. ❸ When soft add in the ginger, coriander, cardamoms, garlic and curry leaves. ❹ Add in the meat and salt. ❺ Stir the ground powder into the meat and fry until meat is brown. ❻ Put the lid on and cook for about 1-1½ hours over a low heat until the meat is cooked. ❼ Add the coconut milk and stir in well. Heat through for about 5 minutes. Enjoy with some plain rice.

Kumi Somadasa
Stirling

TAVA – CYPRIOT BAKED LAMB WITH POTATOES

Serves 6-8

2	Red onions, roughly chopped
1.2kg	Potatoes, cut into large chunks
1kg	Lamb, cut into chunks
4 tbsp	Flat leaf parsley, chopped
3 tsp	Cumin seeds (heaped)
125ml	Olive oil
4-5 ripe	Tomatoes, cut into thick slices
50g	Butter

Preheat oven to 180°C/350°F/Gas Mark 4. ❷ Put the onion, lamb and potatoes into a large ovenproof dish and season. ❸ Add the parsley, cumin seeds and olive oil and mix everything together. ❹ Place the tomato slices on top and dot with butter. ❺ Pour about 125ml water down the sides of the dish. ❻ Cover with foil and cook for about 2 hours, occasionally spooning some of the pan juices over the top. The lamb should be very tender and the potatoes thoroughly cooked. ❼ Remove the foil and increase oven to 200°C/400°F/ Gas Mark 6 and cook for another 45 minutes or so, turning the lamb and potatoes half way through. The meat and potatoes will be browned. Enjoy!!!

This is a simple and delicious recipe and makes an ideal alternative to Sunday roast. Just put everything in a roasting tin and go away and enjoy your day while it cooks. You could use lamb chops if desired.

Shauna Brown
Falkirk

LOIN OF LAMB FILLET WITH A CHILLI AND MINT SALSA

Serves 4

Loin of lamb (ask your local butcher to bone and trim into lamb fillet)
2 Sprigs of thyme
1 Garlic clove
20g Butter
Sunflower oil
Salt and pepper

Salsa:

1½ Green chillies, deseeded and sliced
15 g Mint leaves
3 Spring onions, sliced
1½ Limes, zested and juiced
2 tbsp Sunflower oil
1 dsp Fish sauce
1 dsp Caster sugar

❶ Heat a frying pan, brown and season the lamb in a little sunflower oil. When browned, add garlic, thyme and butter. ❷ Cook meat for about 5 minutes, turning frequently. ❸ When meat is ready, (Think Pink! Pink is good) remove from pan and place on warm plate to rest. ❹ For the salsa put all ingredients into a food processor and blend into a thick sauce.

Thinly slice the lamb into medallions and place onto heated plates. Drizzle the salsa next to the lamb and serve with new potatoes and seasonal green beans.

David MacDonald
Butcher, Drymen

PAN FRIED VENISON LOIN, LYONNAISE POTATOES AND ROAST ROOT VEG WITH A RED WINE SAUCE

Serves 2

Meat:

2 x 6oz Venison loin steaks
Olive oil
Knob of butter
Salt and pepper

Potatoes/Vegetables:

12 Medium baby potatoes, par boiled and sliced
2 Medium red onions, sliced
2 tbsp Butter
2 tbsp Parsley

2 Medium carrots
½ Small turnip
½ Small celeriac
2 tbsp Honey
Olive oil
Knob of butter
Salt and pepper

Sauce:

100 ml Beef stock
1 Glass red wine
1 tbsp Redcurrant sauce
2 tbsp Butter

Meat: ❶ Pan fry the seasoned steaks in a hot pan with olive oil and butter until they are cooked to taste. ❷ Remove and leave to rest for 5 minutes on a warm plate covered with tinfoil. ❸ Deglaze the pan with the beef stock and add the red wine, bring to the boil and reduce by half. ❹ Stir in redcurrant sauce and butter. Potatoes: ❺ In a large heavy skillet melt the butter over a low heat, add the onions and sauté until golden brown. ❻ Add the sliced potatoes and cook for 3-4 minutes, season and add the parsley. Vegetables: ❼ Peel the vegetables and cut into even sized pieces and par boil separately until still crunchy. Refresh in cold water. ❽ Toss in some olive oil and butter, season and add the honey. ❾ Place on a roasting tray and put into a hot oven at 220°C for 8-12 minutes until evenly browned, turning 2-3 times.

Place potatoes in the middle of a warmed plate and place venison on top. Scatter the vegetables around the plate then pour sauce over venison. Enjoy!

Stuart Fraser, Head Chef
Oak Tree Inn, Balmaha

OSSO BUCO

Serves 4

4	Large shin of veal pieces
1	Medium onion, chopped
1	Garlic clove, crushed
2oz	Butter
10fl oz	Dry white wine
12 oz	Tomatoes, peeled and chopped
1 tbsp	Tomato puree
	Salt and pepper

Garnish:

1	Large garlic clove, finely chopped
2 tbsp	Fresh parsley, chopped
1	Lemon, zested

You'll need a wide, shallow flameproof casserole dish that can hold the pieces of veal in 1 layer. ❶ In the casserole dish melt 1oz of butter and fry the onion and garlic until pale gold – about 10 minutes and set aside. ❷ Now add the rest of the butter and fry the pieces of veal to brown on both sides. ❸ Pour over the wine and reduce a little before adding the onion, garlic, tomatoes, tomato puree and seasoning. ❹ Cover the casserole dish and leave it to cook gently on top of the stove for about 1 hour or until the meat is tender and the sauce is reduced. ❺ Before serving, mix the chopped garlic, parsley and lemon zest together, then sprinkle this all over the meat. Serve with rice.

Patti Wood
Airth

CHILLI CON CARNE

Serves 4

50g (2oz) Butter
2 Large onions, finely chopped
2 Garlic cloves, crushed
500g (1lb) Minced beef
2 tsp Chilli powder
4 tsp Ground cumin
55g Tomato puree

2 x 425g (14oz) Tin of red kidney beans, drained
300ml (½ pint) Beef stock
Salt and pepper
Chopped parsley or coriander to garnish
Boiled rice or French bread to serve

❶ Melt butter in flameproof casserole. ❷ Add onions, garlic and fry gently for 5 minutes until golden. ❸ Add the beef and cook, stirring for 10 minutes. ❹ Mix together the chilli powder, cumin and tomato puree and stir into the beef. ❺ Add the kidney beans, stock, salt and pepper to taste. ❻ Cover and cook in a preheated oven at 190°C/375°F/Gas Mark 5 for 15 minutes. ❼ Sprinkle with chopped parsley or coriander and serve hot, with boiled rice or crusty bread.

Ray Heeps
Falkirk

EASY PASTA BAKE

Serves 4-6

500g	Beef mince		200g	Cheese, grated
1	Onion, diced		300g	Penne pasta
100g	Mushrooms, chopped			A little oil
1	Tin of Campbell's condensed tomato soup			Garlic clove (optional)
1	Tin of Campbell's condensed mushroom soup			Mixed herbs or oregano (optional)
				Courgettes or red pepper (optional)

❶ Brown the mince and put in large casserole dish. ❷ Soften the onions in a little heated oil and add to the dish with the chopped mushrooms and stir in the tomato and mushroom soups. ❸ Meanwhile heat a pan of water until boiling and add the pasta. Cook for about 10 minutes, drain and add to dish. ❹ Add extra ingredients as required, give it all a good stir, top with cheese and put it in an oven at Gas Mark 4 for about 35 minutes.

This has been a family favourite for years and now my kids are at university it goes down well with friends/housemates when it is their turn to cook.

Rosemary Sinclair

BOEUF BOURGUIGNON

Serves 4

1lb 8oz (750g)	Rump steak*, cubed
2	Rashers bacon, chopped
2 tbsp	Oil
1 tbsp	Plain flour
12	Shallots
1 tsp	Tomato puree
6oz (180g)	Button mushrooms
	Bouquet garni
1	Garlic clove (optional)
2	Glasses of red Burgundy
¼-½ pt	Stock
	Salt and pepper

❶ Cut meat into 2 inch pieces. Heat oil in frying pan, add the meat and brown quickly but thoroughly on all sides. ❷ Remove and put into casserole dish. (Blanch shallots by placing in cold water and bring to boil for 2 minutes, drain) ❸ Add both bacon and shallots to frying pan and brown slowly. ❹ Draw pan aside, stir in flour and cook for 1 minute. Add to casserole. ❺ Add tomato puree and bouquet garni. Boil wine to reduce a little and add to casserole with half of the stock. ❻ Preheat oven to 175°C/350°F and place casserole in an oven for 1½-2 hours. Serve with boiled rice.

*It is important to use quality steak such as rump and not shoulder steak which is too gristly and sinewy.

Margaret Robertson
Ardrossan

CURRIED SAUSAGES

Serves 6-8

2	Packets of beef sausages
1	Onion
2-3 tbsp	Curry powder
	Beef stock
2	Carrots, sliced
2	Potatoes, cubed
1	Sweet potato, cubed
	Celery, sliced
	Peas
	Cornflour

❶ Parboil 2 packets of beef sausages for 10 minutes. Drain, cool, skin and cut into 4. ❷ Fry an onion and 2-3 teaspoons of curry powder until onions are transparent. ❸ Add sausages and brown. ❹ Add a little beef stock and 2 sliced carrots, 2 cubed potatoes and a cubed sweet potato. ❺ Bring to the boil then simmer. ❻ 20 minutes before serving add celery slices and peas. ❼ Add cornflour to thicken and serve.

This recipe was given to me by my sister-in-law in New Zealand. There are no definite amounts of anything in it, just whatever is at hand!

Note: Any vegetables can be added according to taste and this can be made in vast quantities with with either pork or beef sausages.

Freezes really well.

Fiona Fox
Buchanan Castle, Drymen

MEXICAN RICE

Serves 4

1lb	Steak mince
1	Large tin of tomatoes
4oz	Brown rice
½lb	Onions
1	Red pepper
½ pt	Beef stock
1	Garlic clove
½ tsp	Chilli powder
	Pinch of salt
3oz	Butter
4oz	Breadcrumbs

Preheat oven to 180°C. ❶ Brown the mince in a heavy saucepan. ❷ Gently fry the onions, pepper and garlic in 1oz of melted butter until soft but not coloured. ❸ Add the onion mixture to the mince, along with the tomatoes, stock, chilli powder and salt. ❹ Mix well, add the rice and simmer for approximately 30 minutes, then transfer to an oven proof dish. ❺ Melt the remaining butter and mix with the breadcrumbs. Sprinkle on top of mixture. ❻ Bake in oven until crisp.

Auntie Annie
Lenzie

SPICED BEEF NOODLES

Serves 4

400g	Udon (thick) noodles
400g	Beef fillet, cut into thin strips
2 tbsp	Cornflour
2 tbsp	Sunflower or vegetable oil
1"	Piece of root ginger, peeled and grated
8	Handfuls baby spinach, picked through and washed thoroughly
	Salt and pepper

4	Spring onions, cut in quaters
2 tbsp	Soy sauce
2	Red chillies, seeded and finely sliced (add more or less as you prefer)
4 tsp	Toasted sesame oil
2 tsp	Sesame seeds, toasted lightly in a dry pan for a few minutes

❶ Cook the noodles according to the pack, drain and run under cold water to stop them cooking further. Set aside. ❷ Put the beef strips, cornflour and seasoning into a bowl and toss together. Set this aside too. ❸ Heat the oil in a wok or large pan. ❹ Add the ginger and cook for 30 seconds. ❺ Add the beef and stir fry for 2 minutes or until the meat is just cooked. ❻ Add the spinach, spring onions and 1 teaspoon of water and toss everything until soft. ❼ Add the soy sauce and chilli. Taste and check the seasoning. ❽ Add the noodles and toss everything together really well. ❾ Finally add the sesame oil and seeds tossing 1 last time.

Serve in big bowls with chopsticks for a really informal, fun get-together.

Laurie Paterson
Inverkip

LORNA'S STEAK PIE

Serves 6-8

2lbs Stewing steak
2 Large onions, finely chopped
2 tsp Cornflour
4 tsp Bisto
Salt and pepper
Puff pastry (ready-made)
1 Egg

❶ Brown steak in a large saucepan and add a little water with Bisto. ❷ Bring back to boil, add cornflour then simmer gently for about 1½ hours. ❸ Add chopped onions and seasoning. ❹ Transfer to an oven dish and cover over with pastry. ❺ Use fork to make criss cross lines on top of pastry, brush lightly with beaten egg. ❻ Transfer to preheated oven at 190°C for approximately 20 minutes or until brown. Serve with new or mashed potatoes and selection of vegetables.

Lorna McKerracher

SPAGHETTI BOLOGNESE

Serves 2-3

2 tbsp	Olive oil
1 tsp	Garlic puree
1	Medium onion, finely chopped
3	Rashers unsmoked bacon, chopped
1	Celery stalk, finely chopped
1	Medium carrot, grated
4oz	Mushrooms, sliced
8oz	Lean steak mince
4 tbsp	Tomato puree
1	Glass red wine
2	Tins of chopped tomatoes
1	Beef stock cube
2 tsp	Brown sugar
	Pinch of nutmeg
	Salt and pepper

❶ Heat oil. Add onion, garlic, bacon, celery, carrot and mushrooms. Fry gently for 7 minutes. ❷ Add beef and fry for a further 5 minutes, breaking it up all the time. ❸ Add all the remaining ingredients then cover pan and simmer gently for 45 minutes, stirring occasionally. ❹ Serve with spaghetti, sprinkle over grated Parmesan and freshly ground black pepper.

Aileen Stewart
Dunblane

STOVIES

Medium/large white
potatoes
Small/medium onions
1 Tin of chopped tomatoes
A small amount of stock or
left over gravy
Cooked meat (beef or
lamb are good preferably
left from the day before
roast dinner)

❶ Slice the onions and potatoes into rings and the meat into medium slices.
❷ Place a layer of meat, then onions and potatoes then empty the tinned
tomatoes and gravy into the pan, continue building up the layers depending
on how many you are cooking for. ❸ Then place on the hob at a low heat so
it gently steams for about 2 hours. If you are cooking a large amount it can
take up to 3 hours, cooking time is not critical so it's an ideal dish for late
suppers with friends.

Stovies is a traditional Scottish dish that I was brought up on. There are many
ways to make it but the name comes from the pan it used to be cooked in.
It was a way to incorporate leftover cuts of meat or sometimes just potatoes and
onions, into a meal. Because the meat steams slowly for several hours, it is ideal
for cheaper cuts of meat, leaving them very tender. This is my recipe and you
can add any root vegetables eg carrots and parsnips to the layers depending
on what you have available. Use a large pot with a tight lid.

Christine Johnson
Balfron

CORNED BEEF HASH

Serves 2

1 Tin of corned beef
2 Eggs, beaten
  Beef stock cube eg
  Bovril or Oxo with ½ pint
  boiling water
  Mixed herbs or dried parsley

❶ Break up corned beef with a fork. ❷ Add beaten eggs to stock and pour over corned beef. ❸ Add herbs and put in oven for 30 minutes.

Sheila

ARROZ TAPADO RICE SURPRISE FROM PERU

Serves 4

250g	Lean minced beef
100g	Raisins or sultanas, finely sliced
100g	Kalamata (Greek style) olives, pitted and sliced
1	Medium red onion, finely chopped
2	Hard boiled eggs, chopped in squares
3 tbsp	Vegetable oil
4	Portions of white rice

❶ Heat oil to a high temperature in frying pan. ❷ Fry the meat until it changes colour about 5 minutes. ❸ Add onion and stir allowing it to cook. ❹ When the onion is cooked add the sultanas, olives and water. Boil for 5 minutes on medium heat. ❺ Taste and add salt. ❻ When cooked turn off heat and add the hard boiled eggs. ❼ To serve fill ⅓ cup with cooked rice. Fill the next ⅓ with mince mixture. Top with rest of rice. Turn out of mould with one swift movement. Serve with lettuce leaves and tomatoes.

Solly Georgeson
Drymen

BOBOTIE

Serves 4

1lb	Lean steak mince
1	Small onion
1 tbsp	Apricot jam or marmalade
1 tbsp	Oil
1 tsp	Ground turmeric
1 dsp	Curry powder
1 tsp	Salt
¼ tsp	Pepper
1 tbsp	Chutney
1	Thick slice of bread
2-3 tbsp	Water
1 tbsp	Vinegar
1 dsp	Raisins

Topping:

1	Egg
¼ pt	Milk
	Salt and pepper
	Bay leaf

❶ Heat chopped onion in oil until transparent. ❷ Stir in jam, spices, seasoning and chutney. ❸ Add meat and beat down with back of wooden spoon until loose and browned. ❹ Add bread (which has been soaked in water and squeezed out), vinegar and raisins. ❺ Turn into greased pie dish and level out. ❻ Beat together egg, milk and seasoning and pour over meat with bay leaf. Cook at 180°C/350°F for 20-30 minutes.

Delicious served with some rice, crisp green vegetables and Mrs Ball's Chutney (South African) – available at good supermarkets!

A traditional South African dish and very yummy! A very special reminder of our happy 11 years in South Africa.

Freda Robertson
Buchanan Castle, Drymen

WINTER STEW FROM CANARY ISLANDS

1½lb	Beef or venison, chopped into bite size chunks
1½	Tins of chopped tomatoes
12	Whole cloves
1½	Beef stock cubes
2	Garlic cloves, diced finely
1	Medium onion, finely chopped
	Salt and pepper

❶ Brown meat. ❷ Add all ingredients. Bring to the boil and simmer for 3 hours. I think the flavour is more intense if cooked the previous day or half cooked the night before and finished off on the day of serving.

I personally like the stew served with Dauphinoise potatoes and a green vegetable eg kale or spring greens.

Don't be put off by the garlic it gives a unique flavour and a twist on what is, a pretty normal stew. A nice big glass of red wine goes down nicely with this.

Mairi McGinn
Balmaha

INKY PINKY

Serves 2-4

Take the leftovers from a
typical Sunday lunch:
Cold roast beef, sliced
½ pt Gravy or beef stock
Any root vegetables
1 Onion, sliced
1 tsp Redcurrant jelly/jam
Red wine vinegar to taste

❶ Put all ingredients into a large pot, cover and simmer slowly over a low heat until thoroughly heated through and the onion is soft. ❷ Add a spot of the vinegar to taste and serve with mashed or boiled potatoes.

Cheap and cheerful winter food.

Mr R Alexander
Riverside, Stirling

PENNE CARBONARA

Serves 2

250g	Penne pasta
2	Egg yolks
50ml	Double cream
	Handful grated Parmesan
	Olive oil
	Smoked bacon or
	bacon lardons
	Salt and pepper

1 In a bowl mix cream, yolks, half Parmesan and leave to one side. 2 Bring pot of water to boil, add touch of salt and add penne, boil until al dente about 10-12 minutes. 3 Meanwhile heat large frying pan, add olive oil and bacon, fry until golden. 4 Strain penne reserving some liquid and place back in pot. Add fried bacon with all the juices and egg mixture from the bowl. Do this quickly to avoid eggs scrambling. Serve in bowls with remaining Parmesan sprinkled on top. Season to your taste and scoff!

Ricky Henderson

BAKED LEEK AND BACON RISOTTO

Serves 1

½ tsp	Olive oil
2oz	Leek, sliced
1	Garlic clove
1	Rasher lean bacon
2oz	Risotto rice (eg arborio) (uncooked weight)
	Pinch dried thyme
½	Chicken/beef flavoured stock cube

Preheat oven to 150°C. ❶ Heat the oil in a non-stick frying pan and gently cook the finely sliced leek and crushed garlic until softened. Set aside on a plate. ❷ Add the sliced bacon to the pan and allow to brown. Return the leeks and garlic to the pan and stir in the rice (before adding the rice, measure its volume in a cup or measuring jug) and mix well. ❸ Add the herbs and crumbled stock cube and add 3 times the volume of hot water to rice. Bring to the boil and then transfer to an ovenproof dish. Place high in the oven for 35-40 minutes, until the rice is tender. ❹ Check the dish occasionally and add more water if necessary.

I love it because it can go in the oven unlike most traditional risotto recipes. It is my favourite slimming recipe. Serve a large green salad as a side dish.

Alison Munns
Buchanan Castle, Drymen

VODKA ROSE CREAM RIGATONI

250g Cooked rigatoni or favourite pasta	2 Garlic cloves, pureed
1 Tin of chopped tomatoes (herbs, garlic etc included or fresh)	Lardons, diced
	125ml Vodka
	125ml Single cream
1 Onion	Red pepper flakes (to taste)
1 Red pepper	Seasoning

❶ Sauté lardons, garlic, onion and pepper until vegetables are cooked to desired softness. ❷ Add tinned tomatoes, vodka, cream and red pepper flakes. ❸ Season to taste. Serve over cooked pasta with lashings and lashings of Parmesan cheese!

Caroline Clark
Drymen

POTATO AND BACON BAKE

Serves 4

4	Large potatoes (eg Maris Piper)
250g	Lean bacon (I usually use unsmoked as smoked can sometimes be a bit too salty)
1	Medium onion
1 pt	White sauce (bay leaf can be added to give a bit of extra flavour no need to season sauce)
	Good heap of Cheddar cheese

❶ Thinly slice the potatoes and onion. ❷ Chop bacon. ❸ Layer ingredients into a well buttered/oiled casserole dish starting with potato then onion then bacon until all ingredients are finished always ending with a potato layer. ❹ Pepper can be added but no salt. ❺ Pour over the white sauce to cover (obviously removing bay leaf if used). ❻ Put lid on casserole. ❼ Put in oven at 180°C for 1 hour. ❽ Remove from oven and top with grated cheese, replace lid and put back in oven for further 1 hour, removing lid for final ½ hour. This gives a nice crisp top which my family all fight over!

A nice alternative to the onion is thinly sliced leek and sometimes if I have mushrooms they go in as well.

Elaine Gray
Dunkeld

BACON AND TOMATO PASTA

1	Large onion, chopped
2	Garlic cloves, chopped
1	Pack of bacon, chopped
1	Small tin of tomato puree
½ pt	Chicken stock
2 tbsp	Dark brown sugar
1	Small carton single cream
1	Pack of frozen peas
	Fresh basil
	Pasta

❶ Fry onions and garlic in a little olive oil until soft. ❷ Add bacon and fry for a couple of minutes. ❸ Add tomato puree and fry for a further 5 minutes. ❹ Add sugar and chicken stock and bring to the boil. ❺ Simmer for approximately 10 minutes until reduced. ❻ Add a couple of handfuls of frozen peas and cook for a further 5 minutes. ❼ Add cream and torn up basil and simmer for a few minutes until it looks ready. ❽ Pour sauce over cooked pasta. ❾ Add as much freshly ground pepper and Parmesan cheese as you like.

Easy to make and you don't need to be too exact with any of the ingredients or timings. Courgettes can be substituted for peas, red wine can be substituted for some of the chicken stock and you can miss out the bacon if you want to do a vegetarian option. Obviously best accompanied by a cheeky little Chianti Classico and a bit of Pavarotti!

Christine McConnell
Lenzie

FISH

ROISIN'S FISH PIE

Serves 4-6

1lb	Haddock or cod fillet
½ pt	Milk
2	Bay leaves
10	Peppercorns
1	Onion, sliced
2½oz	Butter
3 tbsp	Plain flour (level)
5fl oz	Single cream

4oz	Cooked prawns (you could also add mussels etc)
2lbs	Potatoes
	Some mushrooms fried in butter
1 cup	Frozen peas or corn or both
	Seasoning

❶ Simmer fish in a pan with milk, bay leaves, peppercorns, onion and salt for about 10 minutes. ❷ Cook and mash potatoes with a little milk and butter. ❸ Remove fish and flake, checking for bones. ❹ Strain liquid and use to make white sauce with 1½oz of butter and the flour. Add in the cream. ❺ Fold fish, prawns, mushrooms and peas or corn into sauce and check seasoning. ❻ Put mixture into a pie dish. Spoon mashed potato over the fish and roughen with a fork. ❼ Bake in an oven at 180°C for 20-30 minutes.

Roisin Munn
Buchanan Castle, Drymen

SMOKED SALMON AND CHIVE PASTA

Serves 4

1 tsp **Extra-virgin olive oil**
350g **(12oz) Fresh pasta bows**
200g **(7oz) Fresh peas**
200g **Tub reduced-fat garlic and herb soft cheese**
250g **(9oz) Smoked salmon, cut into thin strips**
1 tsp **Fresh chives, snipped**
Salt and pepper
Lime wedges and lemon zest, to serve

❶ Bring a large pan of lightly salted water to the boil, add the olive oil and the pasta and cook according to packet instructions. ❷ Add peas for the last 2 minutes of cooking time. ❸ Drain the pasta, then tip back into the saucepan. ❹ Add the soft cheese and stir until melted. ❺ Gently stir in the smoked salmon and a good sprinkling of chives. ❻ Divide the pasta mixture between 4 serving bowls, season with black pepper and serve immediately with lime wedges, lemon zest and another sprinkling of snipped chives.

preparation: 5 minutes
cooking: 10 minutes

Freda Robertson
Buchanan castle, Drymen

ROASTED MONKFISH WITH PROSCIUTTO

Serves 6-8

5oz	Prosciutto or Parma ham
3lb	Monkfish
2	Red and yellow peppers, thickly sliced
4	Courgettes, thickly sliced
1	Large head of garlic, broken into cloves
4 tbsp	Olive oil
1 tbsp	White wine vinegar
2 tbsp	Fresh herbs eg parsley, thyme, oregano, coriander
	Salt and pepper

Stuffing:

1 tbsp	Olive oil
2	Garlic cloves, crushed
1	Medium onion, finely chopped
1oz	Fresh breadcrumbs, toasted
1 tbsp	Fresh parsley, finely chopped

❶ Sauté the onion gently, add garlic, herbs and toasted breadcrumbs. Season. ❷ Lay pieces of string long enough to tie around the parcel on a flat surface. ❸ Arrange prosciutto on top. Place monkfish on top, saving 1 piece. ❹ Layer stuffing onto monkfish, and place remaining fillet on top. ❺ Using the string, roll the ham around the fish parcel and tie up. ❻ Place all the vegetables in a shallow ovenproof dish. Place fish parcel on top. Mix oil, vinegar, herbs with seasoning and drizzle all over the fish and vegetables. ❼ Bake at 190°C/375°F/Gas Mark 5 for 35 minutes basting occasionally. ❽ Allow fish to rest for a few minutes before slicing and serving on a bed of the vegetables.

Delicious with salad and new potatoes.

Elaine Robertson
Glasgow

MALCOLM'S FISH AND RICE

Serves 4

1	Onion
2 tbsp	Olive oil
2	Garlic cloves
2	Tins of tomatoes
200ml	Water
	Basil/oregano to taste
400g	White fish (cod or monkfish is ideal)
25g	Butter
250g	Basmati rice
500ml	Boiling water
200g	Cheddar cheese, grated

❶ Heat the olive oil in a saucepan, finely chop the onion and add it to the pan. ❷ Fry the onion for approximately 10 minutes, stirring occasionally so it doesn't burn. Add the crushed garlic cloves and fry for 3-4 more minutes. ❸ Add the tins of tomatoes, water and herbs and simmer for half an hour until the tomato sauce is thick. Season. ❹ While the tomato sauce is simmering, melt butter in a pan, add the rice, and stir to coat in the butter. ❺ Add the boiling water to the pan, stir, turn the heat down to lowest setting and cover. Leave to cook until all the water has been absorbed into the rice for approximately 15 minutes. ❻ Cut the fish into large cubes and microwave for 3 minutes. Add the fish to the tomato sauce and stir. ❼ Spoon the cooked rice around the edges of a large oblong ovenproof dish. ❽ Add the tomato and fish mixture to the centre. Cover with grated cheese. ❾ Cook in an oven at 180°C for 30-40 minutes or until the cheese is golden and bubbling.

This has become my dad's signature dish. He's been cooking it for about 20 years. When we're visiting home for the weekend and he offers to cook, we know he'll be making this.

Laura Crouchman
Glasgow

RED LENTIL AND PRAWN CURRY

130g	Red lentils – ideally soak in water for 1 hour before needed then rinse
1 pt	Weak vegetable stock
250g	Small prawns
50g	Sachet coconut cream (optional)
	Handful green beans, chopped into 1" pieces
	Coriander or parsley to serve, chopped

Curry Paste:

2	Shallots, finely chopped
3	Fat garlic cloves, finely chopped
2"	Piece of ginger, finely grated
1 tbsp	Cumin seeds
1 tbsp	Coriander seeds
1	Stalk of lemongrass, finely chopped
½	Lime, juiced
	Vegetable oil

❶ Dry fry cumin and coriander seeds then grind to a powder in a pestle and mortar or food processor. ❷ Gently fry the shallots, garlic, ginger, lemongrass in a little oil for 5 minutes. ❸ Add the shallot mixture to the ground seed mix and bash until paste-like. ❹ Add the lime juice to loosen the mixture (a food processor will give similar results). ❺ Heat a little oil in a large pan and gently fry the shallot mixture for 2 minutes. ❻ Add lentils and stock and simmer for 20-25 minutes until lentils are tender (stir frequently and top up with stock to prevent mix drying). ❼ Add beans and prawns and coconut cream (if using) and heat through for a further 5 minutes. ❽ Add coriander and parsley just before serving. Serve with naan bread or chapatis.

This a very fragrant flavoursome curry with no heat. You could add a little (or a lot) of finely chopped red chilli to add heat.

Trish Davidson
Bearsden

TROUT, DILL AND POTATO TART

300g **Shortcrust pastry**
350g **New potatoes, sliced**
284ml **Single cream**
2 **Eggs**
3 tbsp **Dill, chopped (plus extra for sprinkling)**
1 **Lime, zested**
200g **Shetland hot smoked trout, flaked**

Preheat oven to 190°C/Fan 170°C/Gas Mark 5. ❶ Roll out the pastry and line a shallow 28cm flan tin. Trim off the edges, then line with baking paper and beans. ❷ Put on a baking sheet, bake for 10 minutes. Remove the paper and beans and bake for a further 5 minutes. ❸ Cook the potatoes in boiling salted water for 6-8 minutes until tender, then drain. ❹ Beat together the cream, eggs, dill, lime zest, salt and pepper. ❺ Scatter half the potatoes over the bottom of the pastry case and put half the trout in the gaps. ❻ Pour over half the egg mix, then arrange the remaining potatoes over the trout pieces and put the remaining trout in the gaps between. Pour over the rest of the egg mix. ❼ Bake for 25 minutes until the top is lightly coloured and firm to touch. Cool for 10 minutes before removing from the tin. Serve warm, sprinkled with extra dill.

This is from a Shetland friend who owns a health food shop.

Ann Johnson

HADDOCK PIE

Serves 4

2 **Large haddock fillets**
1 **Large smoked**
   haddock fillet
   Grated cheese
   Creamed potatoes
1½ pt **Milk**

❶ Poach the fish in milk. ❶ Once the fish has cooled, flake it into an ovenproof dish, making sure no bones are remaining. ❶ Use the milk from the fish to make a cheese sauce and pour over the fish. ❶ Top the mixture with creamed potatoes and bake in a preheated oven at 180°C/Gas Mark 5 for 35-40 minutes until piping hot. Enjoy.

Any fish can be used eg salmon, trout or a combination of whatever you enjoy.

Gillian Guthrie
Bearsden

MUSSELS PROVENÇALE

Serves 4

1 tbsp	Olive oil
1	Onion, finely chopped
2	Garlic clove, finely chopped
800g	Tin of chopped tomatoes
1kg	(2½lbs) Mussels

❶ In a large pan, add olive oil, then onion and cook until soft. ❷ Next, throw in garlic and cook for a few more seconds on a low heat, be careful not to let onions and garlic get brown. ❸ Tip in tomatoes, bring to the boil, then simmer gently for about 20 minutes. Taste and season with a pinch of sea salt and some ground black pepper. ❹ When ready to serve, tip in prepared mussels, put lid on pan and cook until all mussels open (throw away any that don't). Give the pan a good shake before serving with crusty bread.

Sam Fairhurst
Irvine

SALSA COD

Serves 2

2	Cod steaks
12	Cherry tomatoes
3	Sun blush/dried tomatoes in oil
2	Spring onions, very thinly sliced
2 tsp	Olive oil or hemp oil
2 tsp	Balsamic vinegar
	Large handful fresh basil leaves
	Salt and pepper
5oz	Basmati rice

❶ Cook the rice according to the packet instructions. ❷ Season the cod fillets then arrange the fish on a sheet of baking paper in a steamer. ❸ Mix the rest of the ingredients together (except the basil) in a bowl that will fit in the steamer. Cover the bowl with foil and place in the steamer as well. ❹ Steam everything for about 8 minutes until the fish is cooked (if your fish are large fillets then this may need to be longer). ❺ Split the rice into 2 bowls then serve the fish on top. ❻ Shred the basil leaves and add to the tomato salsa mixture then serve on top of the fish.

This is lovely with other fish such as salmon, or even chicken. You can also add ½ a teaspoon of honey to the tomato salsa before steaming, for a slightly sweeter sauce.

Jacqui Crawford
Glasgow

CHILLI PRAWN LINGUINE

Linguine or tagliatelle
Fresh king prawns (cooked)
1 Red chilli, chopped
1 Garlic clove, crushed
Sunblush Mediterranean
tomatoes
Squeeze of lemon juice
Olive oil

❶ Marinate prawns in all the ingredients except pasta. ❷ Boil Pasta. ❸ Mix prawns through pasta when cooked.

Yvonne Ford
Drymen

THAI FISH

Serves 4

2lb	(900g) Sea bass or similar fish
1 tbsp	Fresh ginger, grated
3	Garlic cloves, finely chopped
½	Onion, finely chopped
2	Red chilli peppers, finely chopped (or 2 dried chilli peppers)
½oz	(15g) Tamarind (optional)
	Groundnut oil
1 tbsp	Soy sauce
1 tsp	Brown sugar
½ tsp	Salt

❶ Clean and trim the fish. Wash and cut into strips. ❷ Place the ginger, garlic, onion and chilli peppers in a food processor and reduce to a paste. ❸ Soften the tamarind in a small bowl of boiling water. When cool, take out the tamarind and rub into the fish fillets gently (optional). ❹ Heat 2 tablespoons of oil in a heavy saucepan and fry the garlic and ginger paste for about 1 minute. ❺ Add the soy sauce, sugar, salt and 2fl oz/50ml water. ❻ Stir, bring to the boil and simmer for a couple of minutes. ❼ Heat enough oil for shallow frying and gently fry the fish fillets for a few minutes. ❽ Take out with a slotted spoon and drain on paper towels. ❾ Transfer to a heated serving platter. Cover with the sauce and serve.

Ann Graham
Buchanan Castle, Drymen

TOMATO RISOTTO WITH GARLIC AND CHILLI PRAWNS

Serves 4

1¼ litres	Chicken stock	1 cup	White wine
3 tbsp	Olive oil		Freshly ground pepper
1	Small onion, finely chopped	20	Prawns
1 tsp	Sea salt	2	Small chillies, chopped
50g	Butter	2	Garlic cloves, chopped
2 tbsp	Tomato paste		Lemon and parsley
1½ cups	Risotto rice		(to serve)

❶ Place stock in a large pot and bring to boil, reduce heat and simmer.
❷ Place large heavy based pan over medium heat and add 1 tablespoon of oil, onion, salt and half of the butter. Stir until onion is soft, add tomato paste and cook for a couple of minutes, stirring. ❸ Add rice, stir 1-2 minutes.
❹ Add wine, stir constantly, slowly adding stock and simmer for 20 minutes.
❺ Remove pan from heat, stir in butter and pepper. Cover and leave for 3 minutes. ❻ Heat remaining 2 tablespoons of oil in frying pan, season prawns and cook for 2 minutes. ❼ Add chilli and garlic and cook for 1 minute.

Serve with prawns on top and some lemon and parsley.

Ellen McKenzie
Dru Yoga Teacher

LINDA'S SALMON IN FOIL

	Fresh noodles
1	Onion
1	Pepper
	Tomatoes
	Herbs
1 tbsp	Sweet chilli sauce
	Salmon slices

❶ Gently sauté onion, pepper, tomatoes and herbs until soft. ❷ Add a tablespoon of sweet chilli sauce. ❸ Place in individual tinfoil parcels with salmon on top. ❹ Bake in oven approximately 20 minutes.

Linda Taylor

SHEILA'S PRAWN SALAD

1 Apple
1 Orange
1 Pear
2 Bananas
1 Tin of mandarin oranges, drained
Walnuts (optional)
Prawns

Sauce:

3 tbsp Mayonnaise
1 Lemon, juiced
1 tbsp Orange juice
1 tsp Sugar
1 tbsp Double cream

❶ Mix salad ingredients. ❷ Mix sauce ingredients and add to salad.

Enjoy!!!

Sheila

KILBRANNAN PRAWN AND ASPARAGUS TARTLETS

Serves 6 – starter/light lunch

6	Large, raw king prawns
12-18	Asparagus tips (2-3 per tart)
3 tbsp	Olive oil
300g	Pack shallots, peeled and quartered
375g	Puff pastry (ready-rolled)
	Splash balsamic vinegar
50g	Pack wild rocket

Marinade and dressing:

6 tbsp	Olive oil
1	Garlic clove, finely chopped
1	Lemon, finely zested
1 tbsp	Parsley, chopped (heaped)

Preheat oven to 220°C/Fan 200°C/Gas Mark 7. ❶ For marinade, mix oil, garlic, zest and parsley, then season. ❷ Marinate prawns and asparagus in half the mixture, stir lemon juice into remainder of dressing. ❸ Heat oil in pan, throw in shallots and seasoning and fry over medium heat for 10 minutes until golden and softened. ❹ Cut out 6 10cm circles from pastry, lay them on a baking sheet. ❺ Using a knife mark a circle part way through the pastry, 1cm in from edge. ❻ Bake for 10 minutes until golden. ❼ Meanwhile, heat a pan, add prawns and asparagus, cook over high heat for 3-4 minutes. ❽ Stir in balsamic, take off heat and add rocket. Spoon shallots, rocket, prawns, asparagus and dressing on top of rounds.

Recommend a nicely chilled bottle of white Sancerre, sun, sand, sea and good company!

Marlene Waudby
Buchanan Castle, Drymen

MONKFISH SCAMPI

Monkfish tails, off the bone
1 **Egg, beaten**
Ruskoline
Groundnut oil

❶ Cut the monkfish into 1 inch chunks. ❷ Dip in beaten egg and then in Ruskoline. ❸ Heat groundnut oil and then fry monkfish pieces until brown and cooked through the centre. ❹ If cooking for a few people, cook in batches and serve fresh to the table or keep warm in a dish in the oven.

Delicious served with lemon mayonnaise and chips for a supper party.

Rhona Baxter
Aberdeen

SPANISH SALMON CASSEROLE

4oz	Quick cooking macaroni
16oz	Tin of salmon
2oz	Grated Cheddar cheese
1oz	Cornflakes
1	Garlic clove, finely chopped
½	Small red or green pepper
1 tsp	Parsley, chopped (level)
½ pt	Milk
2	Eggs, beaten
	Salt and pepper

Topping:

1½oz	Cornflakes
½oz	Cheddar cheese, grated
½oz	Butter, melted
¼ tsp	Paprika pepper (level)

① Cook macaroni according to instructions on packet. ② Drain and flake salmon. ③ Mix together macaroni, salmon, cheese, cornflakes, garlic, finely chopped red or green pepper, parsley, milk, eggs and seasoning. ④ Spread evenly in a greased 2 pint ovenproof dish. ⑤ Topping: In a small basin, mix together finely chopped cornflakes, cheese, butter and paprika. ⑥ Sprinkle over salmon mixture. ⑦ Bake in a moderate oven at 350°F/Gas Mark 4 for about 40 minutes. ⑧ Garnish with parsley. Serve with tomato sauce if desired.

Jill Farquar
Kilmacolm

MICROWAVE LEMON SOLE IN A SAUCE

Serves 4

4	Fillets of sole
¼ pt	Single cream
2oz	Cheese, grated
	Sprinkle of Parmesan cheese
1 tsp	Parsley
½	Lemon, juiced
	Salt and pepper

❶ Skin fish, roll and place in a shallow dish. ❷ Pour cream over, add lemon juice and salt and pepper. ❸ Sprinkle the grated cheese on top, finishing off with the Parmesan. ❹ Cover and cook in the microwave for 3 minutes on high. Sprinkle with parsley and serve.

For special occasions use double cream and grated gruyere cheese.
This makes for an extra rich sauce – delicious!!!

Betty Beith
Buchanan Castle, Drymen

FIONA'S FISH PIE

Serves 4

4 Pieces of haddock
4oz Butter
8oz Cheese
Milk
Salt and pepper
4 Hard boiled eggs
Potatoes, boiled and mashed

❶ Roll fish up with a knob of butter inside. ❷ Place in a pan and cover with milk, season with salt and pepper, bring to the boil and simmer until fish is cooked. ❸ Make up cheese sauce with milk from the cooked fish. ❹ Place the mashed potatoes in bottom of an oven proof dish. ❺ Cut boiled eggs in half and alternate 1 rolled fish, 2 halved eggs. ❻ Cover with cheese sauce and place in a moderate oven until the top is golden brown. Serve with seasonal vegetables and enjoy!

Fiona MacMillan
Rowardennan

WEST COAST SCALLOPS WITH STORNOWAY BLACK PUDDING AND HOLLANDAISE SAUCE

Serves 4

12	Large king scallops
4	Slices Stornoway black pudding
25ml	White wine
100g	Unsalted butter
2	Egg yolks
	Fresh lemon juice
	Chives, chopped

❶ Put egg yolks and wine in a jug. ❷ Heat butter in microwave for 20 seconds. ❸ Use hand blender to quickly mix eggs and wine and slowly pour in warm (not hot) butter. ❹ Squeeze in some fresh lemon juice when mixed. ❺ Grill Stornoway black pudding under grill then rest on a plate. ❻ Season scallops then sear them either side for 2 minutes (maximum). ❼ Add a knob of butter and dash of fresh lemon juice before removing from pan. Do not overcook scallops! ❽ Place Stornoway black pudding in middle of plate with scallops around. ❾ Then, lightly coat with hollandaise sauce. Place under grill for 30 seconds then serve with chopped chives.

Stuart Burch, Head Chef
Wayfarers Restaurant, Croftamie

VEGETARIAN

POTATO AND AUBERGINE BAKE

1kg Potatoes
2 Aubergines
2 Large onions, sliced
250g Cheddar cheese, grated
Seasoning

❶ Slice aubergines and arrange a few in the bottom of a casserole dish.
❷ Cook the onions in oil until soft. ❸ Arrange in layers of aubergine, onion and potato, sprinkling each layer with cheese and seasoning. ❹ Top with cheese and breadcrumbs. ❺ Cover and bake for 1 hour at 190°C or until golden brown.

Sally Windebank
Milngavie

ASPARAGUS TART

200g	(7oz) Asparagus, trimmed
3	Eggs, beaten
150g	(5oz) Crème fraîche
150g	(5oz) Yoghurt
25g	(1oz) Parmesan, freshly grated
20½cm	(8") Shortcrust pastry case (Ready-made)

Preheat oven to 200°C/Fan 180°C/Gas Mark 6 and put in a baking sheet to heat up. ❶ Steam the asparagus over boiling water for 2 minutes. Drain thoroughly. ❷ Put the eggs in a jug and whisk in the crème fraîche, yoghurt and half the grated Parmesan. Season well. ❸ Put the shortcrust case on the baking sheet and pour in the egg mixture until it comes to just below the top of the pastry. ❹ Arrange the asparagus on top and scatter over the remaining Parmesan. ❺ Bake for about 15 minutes, until set.

Kathy O'Donnell
Kippen

BUTTERNUT SQUASH RISOTTO

Serves 4-6

1	Butternut squash
	Olive oil
1	Onion, finely chopped
2	Garlic cloves, chopped
75g	Risotto rice (per person)
1	Glass of white wine
	Chicken stock
30g	Parmesan (per person)
	Slice of butter

❶ Take seeds out of butternut squash, peel, cut into chunks, roast in the oven at Gas Mark 7 with a couple of tablespoons of olive oil on it and some silver foil over the top. Bake for about 45 minutes until cooked. ❷ Fry 1 finely chopped onion in some olive oil on a low heat until soft (15 minutes) add a couple of cloves of chopped garlic and fry for 5 minutes before the end. ❸ Then add risotto rice. ❹ Stir on low heat for 1 minute so the rice is coated, add a glass of white wine if you've got some open, stir. ❺ Meanwhile you've heated up the chicken stock (you really want to use home made stock for this). ❻ Add a few ladles of stock at a time, enough to just cover the rice, stir, cook and add more stock for about 20 minutes. You know it's done when it tastes right. ❼ Take off the heat, add a generous amount of grated Parmesan, a slice of butter, cut into bits (don't think about the calories just do it!) and the butternut squash. Stir briefly. Eat.

We like this with a bit of rocket on the top.

Clara Archer
Drymen

POTATO, CHEESE AND ONION PIE

675g	(1½lb) Potatoes, peeled and thinly sliced
2 tbsp	Olive oil
2	Onions, finely sliced
2	Garlic cloves, chopped
5 tbsp	Double cream
50g	(2oz) Sun-dried tomatoes in oil, drained and chopped
2 tbsp	Fresh parsley, chopped
100g	(4oz) Mature Cheddar, grated
	Shortcrust pastry
1 tbsp	Milk to glaze
	Salt and pepper

Preheat oven to 200°C. ❶ Boil a large pan of water and cook potatoes until tender but not falling apart, drain and leave to dry. ❷ Heat oil in a large pan and cook onions and garlic, covered, until softened and golden. ❸ Add the cream, sun-dried tomatoes and chopped parsley. Season to taste and bring to the boil. Simmer, stirring continuously, until heated through. Leave to cool. ❹ Roll out half the pastry on a lightly floured surface and use to line a 20cm/8 inch spring form cake tin. ❺ Layer half the potatoes in the base, then pour over half the onion and garlic mixture and half the grated cheese. Repeat layers once more. ❻ Brush the pastry edge with water. ❼ Roll out the remaining pastry and cover the top of the pie. Trim the edges and pinch together to seal. ❽ Brush with milk and make a hole in the centre to allow steam to escape. ❾ Place on a baking sheet and bake for 25-30 minutes until crisp and golden.

This pie is a favourite in our house a real comfort food and delicious with steamed vegetables or baked beans.

Sharmi Musgrave
Buchanan Castle, Drymen

SPICY TOMATO PASTA

  2 Tins of organic tomatoes
    Pasta (any type)
 12 Mushrooms
  1 Chilli pepper
    Salt
    Cream
  2 Garlic cloves
  1 Large onion
    Olive oil

❶ Pour 2 tablespoons of olive oil into a large pan and gently heat. ❷ Finely chop onions and add to oil to soften. ❸ Add crushed garlic. ❹ Add chopped chilli pepper and stir together. ❺ Add tomatoes and leave on heat. ❻ Add chopped mushrooms and stir. ❼ In a separate pan boil water for pasta and salt to taste. Add pasta to water and cook. ❽ Turn off heat to sauce and finally add cream and stir. ❾ Drain pasta, add sauce and serve.

Thomas Anderson age 12

EASY QUICHE

4	**Eggs**
½ cup	**Self raising flour**
2oz	**Butter, melted**
2 cups	**Milk**
	Cheese, grated

❶ Preheat oven 180-200°C. Combine all ingredients together, until a batter like consistency. ❷ Add filling of choice – cheese, bacon, mushrooms and pour mixture into a lightly buttered oven proof dish. ❸ Bake for 45 minutes to 1 hour

Gillian Guthrie
Bearsden

PUMPKIN RISOTTO

Serves 2

25g	Butter
1 tbsp	Olive oil
3	Shallots, chopped
½	Butternut squash
175g	Risotto rice
	Handful of frozen peas or soya beans
600ml	Vegetable stock
40g	Parmesan
	Handful of parsley chopped

Preheat the oven to 180°C/Gas Mark 4. ❶ Prepare the squash by cutting in half, scooping out the seeds and cutting the skin off. Cut into large chunks. ❷ Heat the oil and butter in a frying pan. Add the shallots and cook gently for 5 minutes until translucent. ❸ Add squash and cook for a further 5 minutes. ❹ Add risotto rice followed by the stock. ❺ Bring to the boil, stir once then transfer to an ovenproof dish. ❻ Cook uncovered for ½ hour, stirring once after 15 minutes – you can add the peas/beans at this point and you may also need to add some more stock. ❼ Remove from the oven and stir in the Parmesan and parsley. Serve immediately.

You can add chopped raw chicken breast to the pan when frying the squash to make a more substantial meal.

If you don't add salt and pepper and keep the stock weak this makes an excellent meal for children which can be pureed from frozen if needed.

Jacqui Crawford
Glasgow

VEGETABLE AND BEAN JALFREZI

2	Medium sweet potatoes, cut in chunks
½	Small butternut squash, cut in chunks
1	Medium onion, chopped
1	Large courgette, chopped
1	Tin of beans of your choice (eg aduki beans, green lentils, borlotti beans, kidney beans)
1	Jar of Patak's superior spicy jalfrezi sauce
½	Tin of coconut milk
3 tbsp	Vegetable oil
	Chapatis to serve

❶ Heat the oil in a large heavy based saucepan, then add the onion and cook for 5-10 minutes until soft. ❷ Add the sweet potatoes and butternut squash to the pan and fry for a further 5-10 minutes. ❸ Drain and rinse the can of beans and add to the vegetable mixture. ❹ Add the jar of jalfrezi sauce and the coconut milk. Bring to the boil, simmer gently for ½ hour then add the courgettes. ❺ Simmer for a further 30 minutes, stirring occasionally to stop it from sticking to the bottom of the pan. Serve with some warm chapatis.

This can be made more substantial by adding the meat from some cooked skinned chicken thighs and a tin of chopped tomatoes.

This taste even better if refrigerated overnight once cooked and reheated the following day

Jacqui Crawford
Glasgow

HANDY VEGETABLE OPTION

1 Red pepper, chopped
1 Aubergine, part chopped,
  part sliced
  A few cherry tomatoes,
  halved
  Balsamic vinegar
  Extra virgin olive oil

❶ Place pepper and aubergine (or courgette) in a bowl and mix with a small amount of the oil. ❷ Place in a hot oven to roast (approximately 10 minutes). ❸ Place cherry tomatoes in mixture (5 minutes). ❹ Add balsamic vinegar at the end. ❺ When cool place in a covered container and keep in fridge.

Handy with salads.

For filled pitta breads or vegetarian visitors. Spread wrap with humous, add vegetable mixture, wrap. Cut into small servings and use cocktail sticks to hold together.

Ellen McKenzie
Dru Yoga Teacher

CHILLI BEAN CASSEROLE

Serves 6-8

3	Onions, chopped	1 tsp	Coriander
2	Garlic cloves, crushed	1 tbsp	Tomato puree
	Vegetable oil	2	Tins of chopped tomatoes
4	Peppers, deseeded and	4	Tins of assorted beans
	chopped (assorted colours)		(kidney, butter, cannellini,
1	Large red chilli pepper,		flageolet, black eyed)
	deseeded and chopped	¾ pt	Vegetable stock
1 tsp	Chilli powder	1	Glass of red wine (at least!)
1 tsp	Cumin		

❶ Soften the onions, garlic and peppers in the oil. ❷ Add chilli and spices.
❸ Add other ingredients and bring to the boil. ❹ Simmer for 1½ hours.

Serve with cous cous, baked potato or rice, accompanied with grated Cheddar cheese, sour cream and a green salad with avocado.

Dorothy Pattenden
Killearn

ALU GOBI (POTATO AND CAULIFLOWER)

8oz	Potatoes
1 tsp	Turmeric
1	Medium cauliflower
1 tsp	Chilli powder
4oz	Butter or ghee
½ tsp	Cumin seed
¼ tsp	Ginger powder
	Salt to taste
½ tsp	Black pepper

❶ Peel and dice potatoes. Divide cauliflower into florets of the same size. Wash vegetables and drain. ❷ Heat fat, add the potatoes, cumin seed, ginger, turmeric, chilli and salt and fry for 2 minutes. ❸ Add the cauliflower and fry altogether for 5 minutes. ❹ Cover and cook very slowly until tender. ❺ Sprinkle over freshly ground black pepper and serve. No water should be added. ❻ If green ginger is available, use a 1 inch piece sliced very thinly instead of the ginger powder.

Dorothy Senior
Bishop Auckland

RED DRAGON PIE

4oz	Aduki beans		1	Garlic clove, chopped
2oz	Rice		1lb	Potatoes, peeled
2 pt	Water for soaking			and mashed
2 pt	Water for boiling		1oz	Butter
1 tbsp	Oil		1	Onion, finely chopped
8oz	Carrots, grated		1-2 tbsp	Soy sauce
2 tbsp	Tomato puree		1 tsp	Mixed herbs
½ pt	Aduki bean stock			Salt and pepper

❶ Wash Aduki beans and the rice and soak them either overnight or steep in boiling water for 1 hour. ❷ Drain and rinse, then bring to the boil in fresh water and cook for 50 minutes until the grains are fairly soft. Drain, reserving the Aduki liquid. ❸ Heat the oil in the saucepan and fry the onion for 5 minutes, add the carrots and garlic and cook for 2-3 minutes, then add the cooked grains. ❹ Mix the soy sauce, tomato puree and herbs with the stock and pour over the bean and vegetable mixture. Simmer for 20-30 minutes. And season to taste, if required. Add additional stock if mixture seems dry. ❺ Transfer to a pie dish and cover with mashed potatoes. ❻ Bake in the oven at 180°C until top is crispy.

Ali Thompson ·
Buchanan Castle, Drymen

SAVOURY PANCAKES

4oz	Plain flour
	Pinch salt
1	Large egg
½ pt	Milk
1 tsp	Olive oil for mix

❶ Sift flour and salt into bowl, make a well in the centre, add an egg and mix. Slowly add milk until mixture is smooth. ❷ Add olive oil, stir again and leave in fridge for at least an hour. ❸ Heat a dribble of olive oil into a pan. When smoking hot pour in a soup ladle of mixture and roll around pan. Reduce heat if necessary. ❹ When it begins to curl at edges, turn over. ❺ Add filling to a quarter of the crêpe and fold in half, then half again. Turn over to make sure cheese has melted then remove from pan. Filling: ❻ Cheese, ham and mushroom. Grate cheese, slice and cook mushroom before adding to crêpe. ❼ Cream cheese and smoked salmon. Spread cheese over then add pieces of smoked salmon.

Left overs can also be used eg chilli con carne. Serve with salad for a great Shrove Tuesday meal. If you make enough mixture you can have sweet pancakes for dessert. Try with mixed berries and a touch of sherry. Serve with whipped cream.

Bruce Nicol
Hastings

ROASTED VEGETABLES WITH PESTO SPAGHETTI

1 Red bell pepper
1 Yellow or orange bell pepper
   Cherry tomatoes
1 Large red onion
1 Courgette
   A few fine beans, snapped
   into 2-3
   Carrots and mushrooms
   (optional extras)
¼-1 tsp Very Lazy chillies
1-2 Garlic cloves
   Red pesto

❶ Add 1-2 cloves garlic – crushed (or can use Very Lazy garlic), a light sprinkling of cayenne pepper, about ½ a teaspoon of ground cinnamon and a ¼-1 teaspoon of Very Lazy chillies. ❷ Drizzle with olive oil and stir everything well to coat all the vegetables. Cook in the oven at about Gas Mark 5-6, stirring once or twice, until the vegetables are cooked. They usually take about 30-45 minutes. ❸ When vegetables are nearly ready, cook the spaghetti until al dente. ❹ Drain and stir in some red pesto – you need enough to coat the spaghetti, so the volume will depend on how much spaghetti you have made. ❺ Serve the spaghetti into bowls and cover with a generous helping of the roasted vegetables.

This is a quick, easy recipe I knocked together one day and was so tasty it has become a firm favourite. The longest part is preparing the vegetables, so on sunny days I sit in the garden and do them. You can use any vegetables that you like, but this is my usual combination. There are no fixed quantities, just use whatever you have. Incidentally, the roasted vegetables are delicious served with steak or even on toast or crusty bread.

Shauna Brown
Falkirk

ALISON'S PARMIGIANA

Serves 4

1 Large aubergine
1 Jar puttanesca sauce ie tomato/olive/basil sauce
Mozzarella cheese
Strong Cheddar cheese, sliced
A little olive oil

❶ Slice aubergine quite thickly. ❷ Chargrill on both sides in a frying pan – no oil. ❸ Toss in a little olive oil in a 7x9 inch lasagne dish. ❹ Bake on baking sheet in moderate oven for 10 minutes. ❺ Layer aubergine in pasta dish with puttanesca sauce and sliced cheese. Do this twice, ending with sliced Cheddar. ❻ Bake in centre of moderate oven for 15 minutes until topping is golden.

Serve with garlic bread and green salad.

Alison Bruce
Buchanan Castle, Drymen

POTATO SALAD

1kg **Salad potatoes**
2 **Eggs**
1 **Red onion**
Salad cream
1 tsp **Sugar (level)**
Salt and pepper

❶ Boil the potatoes leaving a little harder than normal. Leave to go cold then dice.
❷ Hard boil the eggs, cool in cold water, then break up with a fork. ❸ Finely dice
the onion. ❹ Mix all together then add the sugar, salt and pepper. ❺ Add salad
cream to taste and mix gently preferably with a plastic tool to avoid breaking up
the diced potato.

George Arkless

SPICED ONION

1	Large onion
3-4 tbsp	Tomato sauce
¼ tsp	Mint sauce
	Chilli powder
	Pinch salt

❶ Dice onion and add salt. ❷ Mix sauces with chilli powder (to taste). ❸ Combine the sauce with the onions and get stuck in!

Gillian Guthrie
Bearsden

KUMI'S SPICY POTATOES

1 lb	New potatoes, peeled and in ½" cubes
1	Red onion, finely diced
6	Bay (curry) leaves
½ tsp	Turmeric
¾ tsp	Ground red chilli
3 tsp	Corn/olive oil
¾ tsp	Maldon salt

❶ Place potatoes in a pan and just cover with water. Add salt, and turmeric.
❷ Boil potatoes gently until firm but cooked. Drain the water into another container.
❸ Heat a frying pan and add the oil. Add the potatoes and the chilli powder.
❹ Fry gently until there is a coating on the potatoes. ❺ Then add the onion and fry until opaque. If the potatoes stick add a bit more oil. ❻ Then add a little of the remaining water and scrape the bottom. Repeat this until the water in the frying pan has evaporated. You do not need to use all the remaining water. Take off heat and let it cool.

Kumi Somadasa
Stirling

SIMPLE PANEER

500g **Paneer, cubed**
30-35g **Poppy seeds**
Salt to taste
½ tsp **Sugar**
1 tbsp **Vegetable oil**

❶ Grind the poppy seeds to a paste and set aside. ❷ Heat the oil in a pan and lightly fry paneer, add poppy seed paste, salt, and sugar. ❸ Fry for a few minutes. Serve hot with chappatis.

Ujani Andrews

SWEET POTATO SALAD

Serves 4

2	Large sweet potatoes
3	Spring onions, chopped
¼ cup	Mayonnaise
½ cup	Sour cream
½ tsp	Curry powder
	Salt
1 tbsp	Walnuts, chopped

❶ Cook sweet potato in boiling, salted water until just tender. Drain and leave to cool. Cut into 2½cm cubes. ❷ Combine the sweet potato and spring onions in a serving bowl. ❸ In another bowl, combine mayonnaise, sour cream, curry powder and salt to taste. ❹ Pour this over sweet potato and mix well. Garnish with walnuts.

Fiona Fox
Buchanan Castle, Drymen

CONDIMENTS

LEMON CURD

4 **Large lemons, zested and juiced**
4 **Large eggs**
200g **Unsalted butter**
300g **Caster sugar**

❶ Whisk the eggs in a medium-sized saucepan, then add the rest of the ingredients and place the saucepan over a medium heat. ❷ Now stir continuously over the heat until the mixture thickens – about 7-8 minutes. ❸ Next, lower the heat to its minimum setting and let the curd gently simmer for a further minute, continuing to whisk. After that, remove it from the heat. ❹ Now pour the lemon curd into the sterilised jars, cover straightaway with waxed discs, seal while it is still hot and label when it is cold. It will keep for several weeks, but it must be stored in a cool place.

It's very easy to do and you can replace the lemons with other fruit such as oranges, limes, passion fruit for alternative flavours. Bearing in mind that an orange will have much more juice than a lemon. Great on thick slabs of white bread or as a filling for sponge cakes.

I used to make this as a kid for my mum on mothers day because I had no money and it has now become a tradition to give her some lemon curd every year.

Clare Laidlaw

APRICOT CHUTNEY

6 pounds

1 lb	Dried apricots, chopped
1½ lb	Onions
8 oz	Sultanas
1 pt	White malt vinegar
2	Oranges, zested and juiced
2 tsp	Salt (level)
1 tsp	Turmeric (level)
½ tsp	Ground cinnamon (level)
1 tbsp	White mustard seeds
1 lb	Soft light brown sugar

❶ Add all ingredients to saucepan, apart from half the vinegar and all the soft brown sugar. Simmer for 30 minutes. ❷ Mix the vinegar into the brown sugar and stir to dissolve. ❸ Once ingredients have simmered for 30 minutes add vinegar and sugar to the pan and simmer for a further 2 hours making sure that you keep stirring quite often to stop it sticking. ❹ Once thickened, take off heat and put into warmed jars.

Lorna Cranston

CAESAR SALAD DRESSING

1	Egg yolk
	Fresh ground pepper
	Garlic, crushed and finely chopped
1 tsp	Dijon mustard
	Anchovy paste
1 dash	Worcester sauce
½	Lemon, juiced
3-4 tbsp	Vegetable oil
	Romaine lettuce
	Parmesan cheese
	Croutons

❶ Mix together all ingredients except oil, lettuce, cheese and croutons with the bottom of a large spoon and crush together as you mix. ❷ Slowly add vegetable oil. When thoroughly mixed, add chopped dry romaine lettuce and Parmesan cheese and croutons to finish.

Enjoy!

This recipe came from a friend in Key West.

Val McDonald
Drymen

CRAB DIP

16oz Sour cream
1 Tub of cream cheese
2 Tins of crabmeat
1lb Shrimp
Old Bay seasoning
(or any seafood seasoning)
½ Lemon, juiced
Splash of tabasco
White pepper

❶ Mix together by hand or with a blender. ❶ Great to serve to a crowd before a barbecue or supper with some good quality crisps.

Rhona Baxter
Aberdeen

BEETROOT CHUTNEY

4lb	Cooked beetroot (buy 5lb and weigh after cooking)
2lb	Cooking apples (buy 3lb and weigh after peeling and dicing)
2	Large onions
1½ pt	Vinegar
1½lb	Demerara sugar
1 tsp	Ground ginger

❶ Cook beetroot and leave to cool. ❷ Chop onion and apples and cook slowly in vinegar and ginger for 20 minutes. ❸ Add chopped up and cooked beetroot with sugar and cook slowly for a further 20 minutes. ❹ Put in sterilised jars. When cool put lids on jars.

Marina Brennan
Drymen

FREDA'S SEVILLE MARMALADE

Makes 20lb

2lb	Bitter Seville oranges
2	Lemons
10lb	Cane sugar
20 Cups	Cold water

❶ Cut fruit into quarters and remove pips over a bowl to catch the juice. Keep pips. ❷ Put orange and lemon quarters through a food processor and put in jelly pan with any surplus juice from stage 1. ❸ Place pips in a small pot with 2 of the 20 cups of water and bring to boil and simmer gently over low heat for 15 -20 minutes. ❹ Add 18 cups of water to jelly pan. Bring to boil and boil for further 30 minutes. ❺ Add liquid from pips. ❻ Take jelly pan off the heat and add sugar slowly whilst stirring all the time. ❼ Return jelly pan to heat and stir until it returns to the boil. Time for 15 minutes then do 1st test to check if set. ❽ If set add a small knob of butter to remove scum before pouring into sterilised jars.

This marmalade has won prizes at Buchanan Flower Show!

Freda Robertson
Buchanan Castle, Drymen

SPINACH-FILLED PUMPERNICKEL

1 Round pumpernickel (dough bun)
1oz Packet frozen spinach, chopped
1 cup Mayonnaise
1 cup Sour cream
1 Medium onion, chopped
1 Packet of vegetable soup

❶ Thaw spinach and drain well until barely moist. ❷ Combine with mayonnaise, sour cream, onions and soup... mix and stir well. ❸ Cover and chill for several hours. ❹ Slice top third off pumpernickel and remove bitesize pieces of bread. Fill hollowed bun with dip.

Serve with pieces of pumpernickel, raw vegetables and crackers.

Ashleigh Robertson
Buchanan Castle, Drymen

TOMATO, ONION AND GREEN CORIANDER RELISH

Serves 4-6

½ lb (225g) Tomatoes
3oz (75g) Onion, peeled
4 tbsp Fresh corriander, chopped (heaped)
¾ tsp Salt
2 tbsp Lemon juice
½ tsp Cayenne pepper
½ tsp Ground roasted cumin seeds (optional)

❶ Cut tomatoes and onions into ¼ inch cubes and put into small non-metalic dish. ❷ Add all other ingredients and mix.

Superb with curry.

Freda Robertson
Buchanan Castle, Drymen

BAKING

WHEATEN BREAD

Makes 2-3 loaves

400g	(14oz) Wheaten meal
175g	(6oz) Wholemeal
110g	(4oz) Plain flour
2 tsp	Baking soda
2 tsp	Salt
50g	(2oz) Caster sugar
50g	(2oz) Margarine
1pt	Buttermilk

Preheat oven 200°C/400°F/Gas Mark 6. Cooking time approximately 25 minutes/1lb tin ❶ Rub margarine into dry ingredients. ❷ Add buttermilk. ❸ Mix together. Turn mixture into a 2lb loaf tin or 3 x 1lb loaf tins and cook until bread sounds hollow when tapped.

This is delicious served with smoked salmon, cream cheese, pâté, and even marmalade at breakfast time. (See Freda's Seville marmalade!) Wheaten bread is a firm favourite of Northern Ireland people – where I come from originally!

Freda Robertson
Buchanan Castle, Drymen

BARA BRITH (SPECKLED BREAD)

Makes 1 loaf

300g	Mixed fruit (raisins, sultanas and chopped apricots)
75g	Raw brown sugar
½	Lemon, zested
400ml	Hot strong tea
200g	Plain flour
150g	Wholemeal flour
2 tsp	Baking powder
2 tsp	Mixed spice
1 tbsp	Marmalade
1	Free range egg, beaten

❶ Mix the fruit, sugar and lemon zest with the hot tea, cover and leave to soak overnight. ❷ Next day strain the fruit and keep the liquid. ❸ Combine the remaining ingredients in a mixing bowl and add the soaked fruit. ❹ Slowly add enough liquid to mix to a soft 'dropping' consistency. ❺ Pour into a greased and lined 900g (2lb) loaf tin. Bake in the oven at 190°C/375°F/Gas Mark 5 for about 50 minutes, until risen and firm to the touch. Leave to cool in tin for 5 minutes then remove and leave to cool on wire tray. Serve sliced with real butter.

Rachel Murray
Powys, Wales

RICH JAMAICAN LOAF

Makes 2 loaves

75g	(3oz) Margarine
125g	(4oz) Light soft brown sugar
1 tbsp	Syrup
1 tbsp	Black treacle
2	Medium eggs, beaten
225g	(8oz) Banana, mashed
225g	(8oz) Self raising flour
1 tsp	Mixed spice (level)
¼ tsp	Bicarbonate of soda (level)
½ tsp	Salt (level)
225g	(8oz) Raisins
1 dsp	Warm syrup (for glazing)

Preheat oven to 160°C/325°F/Gas Mark 4. Line 2 loaf tins 19cmx9cm (1lb loaf tin) with greaseproof paper or use a loaf tin liner. ❶ Cream margarine and sugar until light and fluffy. ❷ Stir in syrup and treacle. ❸ Add eggs and banana to creamed mixture. ❹ Sieve flour, spice, bicarbonate of soda and salt and add to mixture along with the raisins. Mix well. ❺ Divide mixture equally between the 2 prepared tins. ❻ Bake in preheated oven for 45-50 minutes until well risen and firm to the touch. ❼ Remove from loaf tin and brush with warm syrup. ❽ Cool on wire tray then store in airtight tin.

Helen MacLeod
Croftamie

CANADIAN LOAF

Makes 1 loaf

1 cup	Sugar
1 cup	Water
1 cup	Mixed fruit
1 tsp	Mixed spice
1 tsp	Ground ginger
1 tsp	Cinnamon
1 tsp	Bicarbonate of soda
3oz	Margarine
2 cups	Self raising flour
1	Egg

❶ Bring all ingredients except flour and egg to the boil slowly and boil for 5 minutes. Cool the mixture. ❷ Add 2 cups of self raising flour, 1 egg and mix. ❸ Pour the mixture into a 2lb loaf tin. ❹ Bake in a moderate oven 350°F/ Gas Mark 4 for 1 hour.

This is a recipe I have used for many years and I usually make it in batches of 3 as they freeze well. More recently, both my daughter and I have experimented successfully with making it without the egg and also using dairy-free spread instead of margarine to make a dairy-free cake.

Maureen Dorward
Aberdeen

BELGIAN LOAF

Makes 1 loaf

1 cup	Sultanas
1 cup	Sugar
1 cup	Milk
4oz	Margarine
2 cups	Plain flour
½ tsp	Bicarbonate of soda
½ tsp	Baking powder
1	Egg

❶ Melt the sultanas, sugar, milk and margarine in a pan and bring to the boil and allow to cool. ❷ Add contents of pan to flour and dry ingredients. ❸ Add an egg. Mix together. ❹ Bake in a greased loaf tin for 1 hour 325°F/Gas Mark 3.

Nancy Lees
Falkirk

WALLABY LOAF

Makes 1 loaf

8oz	Self raising flour
2	Eggs, beaten
1 cup	Granulated sugar
1 cup	Cold water
1 tsp	Bicarbonate of soda
1 tsp	Cinnamon
½lb	Mixed fruit
¼lb	Stork margarine

❶ Put fruit, water, sugar, margarine and bicarbonate of soda into a saucepan and bring to the boil, simmer for 10 minutes. ❷ Remove from heat and allow to cool. ❸ Once cool, add beaten eggs, sieved flour and cinnamon. ❹ Pour into a well greased 2lb loaf tin and bake in a moderate oven at 180°C/350°F/Gas Mark 4 for around 45 minutes.

Allow to cool before turning out and slicing.

Ruth McDiarmid
Dunblane

YOGHURT LOAF

Makes 2 loaves

150g Natural Yoghurt
1 Vegetable oil
2 Caster sugar
3 Self raising flour
3 Eggs

❶ Beat all the ingredients together and put in 2 x 1lb tins. ❷ Bake 180°C/350°F/ Gas Mark 4 for 45 minutes.

J.M. Fotheringham

CHOCOLATE AND VANILLA LOAF CAKE

Makes 1 loaf

175g	Caster sugar
½ tsp	Vanilla essence
225g	Self raising flour, sieved
50g	Dark chocolate
175g	Butter or soft margarine
3	Eggs
	Icing sugar

Preheat oven to 190°C. Lightly grease 450g loaf tin. ❶ Beat all the ingredients together until light and fluffy. Beat in vanilla essence. ❷ Gradually add the eggs, beating well after each addition. ❸ Carefully fold in self raising flour. ❹ Divide the mixture in half. ❺ Melt dark chocolate and stir into half of the mixture until well combined. ❻ Place vanilla mixture in the tin and level the top. Spread the chocolate layer over the vanilla layer. ❼ Bake in preheated oven for 30 minutes or until springy to the touch. Leave to cool in the tin for a few minutes before transferring to a wire rack to cool completely.

Serve the cake dusted with icing sugar.

Hazel Hill
Killearn

DATE AND SULTANA LOAF

Makes 1 loaf

½ cup	Dates, chopped
½ cup	Sultanas
1 cup	Milk
1 cup	Light brown sugar
125g	Butter or margarine
2½ cups	Self raising flour
2	Eggs, beaten

❶ Grease and line a loaf tin. ❷ Put fruit, milk, sugar and margarine in a pan. Bring to the boil and take off heat. ❸ Let mixture cool slightly. ❹ Beat in flour and egg. Pour into lined tin. ❺ Bake in preheated oven for 45 minutes at Fan 150°C until golden and firm.

This recipe has been a favourite in my husband's family for many years. It always turns out well!

Amanda Forbes
Killearn

BANANA LOAF

Makes 1 loaf

- 75g **Butter**
- 175g **Caster sugar**
- 2 **Eggs**
- 275g **Bananas, skins removed**
- 225g **Plain flour**
- 3 tsp **Baking powder (level)**
- 50g **Walnuts, roughly chopped**

❶ Cream butter until soft, then work in sugar. ❷ Add eggs and beat to a smooth mixture. ❸ Mash bananas well, add to egg mixture and beat until blended. ❹ Sieve flour and baking powder, and stir until mixed. ❺ Add nuts and stir again. ❻ Turn mixture into a well greased loaf tin measuring 9x5x2½ inches. ❼ Bake at 180°C/350°F/Gas Mark 4 for 1-1¼ hours.

Patricia Roxburgh
Gartocharn

MAYO MICROWAVED CHOCOLATE CAKE

Makes 4 cakes

240g	Plain flour
60g	Cocoa powder
2 tsp	Baking powder
1 tsp	Bicarbonate of soda
2	Large eggs, beaten
260g	Caster sugar
250ml	Mayonnaise (not light)
250ml	Water
1 tsp	Vanilla essence

❶ Sift flour, cocoa, baking powder and bicarbonate of soda together. ❷ Beat egg and sugar together. ❸ Fold the liquid into the dry ingredients and add mayonnaise, water and essence to the mixture. It will be very runny! Don't panic. ❹ Use a shallow microwave suitable bowl at least 5cm deep and 14cm in diameter. Wet a sheet of kitchen towel and line the bowl. ❺ Pour in the mixture to about 1cm below the rim. Place in microwave for 5 minutes on high. Test and if still sticky on top – microwave for further batches of 30 seconds testing after each 30 seconds blast. ❻ Once cooked – turn out and peel off kitchen paper. I find this mix makes me 4 such cakes and I do not use a bigger bowl so that the cakes are cooked through. ❼ Slit and use filling of choice. One of my favourites is cream whipped with some icing sugar and some toasted oatmeal added to it. I use this as a thin sliver for a filling then on top and grate some dark chocolate curls on top of the cream as a garnish.

Laura E. Alexander
West Kilbride

BANANA BUTTER CAKE

Makes 1 cake

4	Medium bananas
250g	Self raising flour
2 tsp	Baking powder (level)
100g	Butter
200g	Caster sugar
2	Eggs

❶ Grease and line 2 x 1lb loaf tins. ❷ Measure all ingredients into a bowl and beat until smooth. ❸ Spoon half the mixture into each tin. ❹ Bake for 45 minutes at 180°C.

Ruth Tainton

'TO DIE FOR' LEMON CAKE

Makes 1 cake

100g	Margarine or butter
175g	Caster sugar
2	Eggs, lightly beaten
175g	Self raising flour
30-75ml	(2-5 tbsp) Milk
1	Lemon
75g	Icing sugar

① Cream the margarine and caster sugar. ② Add eggs and zest of a lemon.
③ Then gradually add the flour and milk to the mix. ④ Bake for 1 hour at 180°C
⑤ Remove from oven and spike all over with knitting needle (saved for village
show handcrafts stall!) ⑥ Dissolve icing sugar in lemon juice and pour it over
the cake. Take out of tin when cold

Ruth Tainton

APRICOT AND GINGER SLICE

250g Butter
300g Rich tea or digestive
      biscuits, crushed
200g White chocolate buttons
100g Dried apricots, chopped
100g Crystallised stem ginger,
      chopped
397g Tin of condensed milk

Preheat oven to 200°C/Fan 180°C/Gas Mark 6. Grease and line a 9½x14½ inch (approximately) tray with non-stick parchment. ❶ Melt butter and stir in biscuit crumbs mixing well. Press firmly into tray. ❷ Sprinkle white chocolate buttons over the base, followed by the apricots and ginger. ❸ Drizzle the condensed milk on top. ❹ Put in centre of oven for 20 minutes.

Leave in tray to cool before cutting into small slices. Enjoy!!!

Dorothy Murrison
Milngavie

DELICIOUS APPLE CAKE

Makes 1 cake

225g (8oz) Self raising flour
150g (5oz) Butter, melted
1 tsp Baking powder (level)
350g (12oz) Cooking apples
25g (1oz) Flaked almonds
3 Large apples, peeled and cored
225g (8oz) Caster sugar
2 Eggs
½ tsp Almond essence

❶ Grease 8oz loose-bottomed cake tin. ❷ Place flour, baking powder, sugar, eggs, almond essence and melted butter into bowl, mix well and beat for 1 minute. ❸ Spread half mixture into the tin. ❹ Thickly slice apples and pile on top. ❺ Spoon remaining mixture over apples and top with flaked almonds. ❻ Cook at 160°C/325°F for 1½ hours.

Ruth Tainton
Edinburgh

CARROT CAKE

Makes 1 cake

6oz	Self raising flour
6oz	Sugar
½ tsp	Cinnamon
½ tsp	Mixed spice
½ tsp	Salt
½ tsp	Bicarbonate of soda
4 fl oz	Vegetable oil
2	Eggs
1 cup	Carrots, grated
½	Large tin of crushed pineapple (or small tin of pineapple chunks mashed)

Icing:

3oz	Philadelphia cheese
8oz	Icing sugar

❶ Sieve the dry ingredients together. ❷ Mix oil and egg together and then add to the dry ingredients. ❸ Add carrots and pineapple and mix well. ❹ Pour into a greased 7-8 inch tin. ❺ Bake for 45-60 minutes at 180-190°C/Gas Mark 4-5. ❻ Icing: Beat cheese and add sugar mixing well. Ice cake when cool.

This is a foolproof recipe for carrot cake which I was given by a school friend 20 years ago.

Chloe Rankin
Croftamie

FIG AND APPLE CAKE

Makes 1 cake

8oz	Unsalted butter, room temperature
8oz	Golden caster sugar
1 tsp	Vanilla extract
4	Large eggs, beaten
8oz	Self raising flour
4 tbsp	Milk
2 tsp	Baking powder
9oz	Dried figs, chopped˙
14oz	Cox's apples, peeled cored and chopped
3 tsp	Cinnamon
1oz	Flaked almonds to decorate

Preheat oven to 180°C/Fan 160°C. Line a 12x9 inch roasting tin with greaseproof paper ❶ Using either a wooden spoon or an electric hand whisk, beat together the butter, sugar and vanilla until pale. ❷ Add the eggs a little at a time and then the flour. ❸ Add milk. ❹ Sift together the flour and baking powder and fold in. If thick add more milk. ❺ Add the figs, apples and cinnamon. ❻ Spoon into lined tin and sprinkle almonds on top. ❼ Bake for 35-40 minutes.

˙Chopped, dried apricots can be used instead of figs.

Carol Miller
Gleneagles

ALMOND, LEMON AND HONEY CAKE

Makes 1 cake

350g	Butter
250g	Caster sugar
	Pinch of salt
4	Eggs
200g	Ground almonds
100g	Wholemeal self raising flour
1 tsp	Baking powder
1	Lemon, zested
50g	Flaked almonds
4 tbsp	Runny honey
1	Lemon, juiced

Preheat oven to 160°C. Grease 24cm diameter tin and sprinkle with flour. ❶ Cream together the butter, sugar and salt in a large bowl. ❷ Add the eggs, almonds, flour, baking powder and lemon zest. ❸ Pour mixture into baking tin. Sprinkle almonds on top and bake for 45 minutes. ❹ Mix honey, lemon juice and warm. Spoon over warm cake. Serve warm with crème fraîche.

Antje Peters

APPLESAUCE CAKE

Makes 1 cake

290g	Plain white flour
½ tsp	Ground allspice (optional)
370g	Granulated white sugar
1½ tsp	Baking soda
1½ tsp	Salt
¼ tsp	Baking powder
¾ tsp	Ground cinnamon
475g	Jar Bramley apple sauce (chunky, not smooth apple sauce)

½ cup	Water
½ cup	(75g) Shortening (Cookeen, butter or margarine), melted
2	Eggs
1 cup	Raisins
½ cup	Walnuts, chopped (optional)

Preheat oven to 180°C/Fan 160°C/350°F. Thoroughly grease and then lightly flour oblong baking tin 13x9x2 inches, or 2 round layer tins 8 or 9x1½ inches. (This will be a very dense mixture, so you should avoid using a small deep tin; a larger tin will produce a better cake.) ❶ Put all dry ingredients in a large bowl and mix well with a wooden spoon. ❷ Make a well in the dry mixture, then put all the wet ingredients in. ❸ Mix well again until all ingredients are thoroughly mixed, then add raisins and walnuts. Pour into prepared tin(s). ❹ Bake until wooden pick inserted into centre of cake comes out clean: oblong 55 minutes, layers 45 minutes. ❺ Allow to cool in tin completely before cutting and then remove from tin. (Note if your oven runs hot, then decrease cooking temperature accordingly.)

Kathy O'Donnell
Kippen

TORTA DI POLENTA

Makes 1 cake

- 100g **Shelled almonds**
- 75g **Italian 00 flour or strong bread flour**
- 2 tsp **Baking powder**
- **Pinch of salt**
- 125g **Unsalted butter, softened**
- 125g **Caster sugar**
- 2 **Medium eggs and 2 egg yolks**
- 100g **Polenta flour (maize)**
- **Butter and dried breadcrumbs for the tin**

180°C/350°F/Gas Mark 4 ❶ Put the skinned almonds on a baking tray and toast them for 10 minutes. ❷ Sift the flour with baking powder and salt. ❸ Beat the butter and sugar until smooth. ❹ Lightly beat the eggs and yolks together and add to the butter-cream by the spoonful alternately with spoonfuls of the sifted flour mixture. ❺ Grind the almonds with a couple of tablespoons of polenta flour then add to the cake mixture together with the remaining polenta flour. Mix well. ❻ Butter a loaf tin 17x5cm. ❼ Sprinkle in a couple of tablespoons of breadcrumbs to coat the tin. Spoon the cake mixture in and bake for 45 minutes. ❽ Sprinkle icing sugar on top before serving.

This is a traditional recipe from the North of Italy. It is ideal for afternoon tea.

Luisella Mosley

CAN'T GO WRONG CHOCOLATE SPONGE

Makes 1 cake

6oz	Granulated sugar
6oz	Margarine
3	Eggs
6oz	Self raising flour
2oz	Drinking chocolate powder
1 tsp	Icing sugar

❶ Mix together sugar, margarine and eggs in mixer. ❷ Add flour, drinking chocolate powder and a dash of water. Mix together for a couple of minutes. ❸ Line baking tray with baking paper. ❹ Add mix and put in preheated oven at 350°F (fan assisted) for approximately 20 minutes. ❺ Sprinkle icing sugar once cake has cooled and serve.

Hannah Taylor

DUMPLING

Makes 1 dumpling

8oz	Self raising flour
8oz	Dried fruit
1	Egg
	Pinch of salt
1 tsp	Baking powder
3oz	Atora beef suet
2 tbsp	Syrup or treacle
1 tbsp	Demerara sugar
	Water to soft dough

❶ Grease bowl with butter and demerara sugar. ❷ Mix all ingredients together and pour into bowl for steaming. ❸ Place sheet of baking paper over top of bowl and secure with string. ❹ Put bowl into a pot of boiling water. Simmer for 2½ hours.

This is a recipe that was served daily from Knotts Restaurant in Florence St, Gorbals between 1930 and 1952. A favourite dish of Benny Lynch, World Champion Boxer

Hannah Taylor

APPLE CAKE

Makes 1 cake

225g	Cooking apples, peeled, cored and chopped
225g	Sultanas
150ml	Milk
175g	Soft brown sugar
350g	Self raising flour
2 tsp	Mixed spice (level)
1	Egg, beaten
25g	Demerara sugar

❶ Mix together the apples, sultanas, milk and sugar. ❷ Sieve together the flour and spice, then rub in the butter. ❸ Add the fruit mixture and egg. Mix well. ❹ Place in a buttered and lined 20cm square cake tin. Sprinkle with demerara sugar and bake in the oven at 170°C/Gas Mark 3 for 1¾ hours, until risen and golden brown.

Very moreish!!!

Terri O'Neill
Berkhamstead

SUPER CHOCOLATEY CUPCAKES

Makes 12 cupcakes

100g	Milk or plain chocolate chips
200g	Self raising flour, sieved
200g	Light muscovado sugar
4 tbsp	Cocoa
150ml	Sunflower oil
100ml	Natural yoghurt
2	Eggs
1 tsp	Vanilla extract

Icing:

100g	Plain chocolate
50g	Butter
50g	Icing sugar

Preheat oven to 180°C and line a 12 hole muffin tin with paper cases. ❶ Put the flour, sugar, cocoa, oil, yoghurt, eggs and vanilla extract into a large mixing bowl and whisk together until smooth. ❷ Stir in the chocolate chips. ❸ Divide the mixture between the cases and bake in the oven for 20 minutes, until a skewer inserted comes out clean. Cool on a wire rack. ❹ Icing: Melt the butter and chocolate together. ❺ Sieve the icing sugar into the chocolate and butter mixture and stir until smooth and thick.

Laura Shand
Gartocharn

MICROWAVE DUMPLING

Makes 1 dumpling

½ pt	Water
¾ cup	Sugar
¾lb	Mixed fruit
½lb	Margarine
1 tsp	Mixed spice

❶ Put all ingredients in a saucepan and bring to the boil. ❷ Immediately add ½lb plain flour, 2 eggs and ½ a teaspoon of bicarbonate of soda. ❸ Line a bowl with cling film and add mixture. ❹ Microwave for 9 minutes on full power. ❺ Stand for 2 minutes and turn out.

Rae Heeps
Falkirk

MRS FERGUSON'S CAKE

Makes 2 cakes or 24 buns

6oz **Self raising flour**
4oz **Margarine**
6oz **Caster sugar**
1½ tsp **Baking powder**
3 **Large eggs**

Icing:

10oz **Icing sugar**
2oz **Butter**
4 tbsp **Milk**
A dash of vanilla essence (you can add 4 tbsp fresh orange juice instead of milk and vanilla). You can make icing stiffer or softer as desired.

Preheat oven to 160°C for 25-30 minutes. ❶ Put all ingredients in bowl and mix until smooth and creamy. ❷ Put in 2 cake tins or 24 small cakes. ❸ In a bowl mix the icing sugar, butter, milk and vanilla essence. Then ice the cakes.

This is from an old neighbour of my Gran's and it never fails!

Val Sneddon

ROD'S CARROT CAKE

Makes 1 cake

12oz	Plain flour
2 tsp	Baking powder
1½ tsp	Baking soda
½ tsp	Salt
4	Eggs
1 cup	Vegetable oil
1lb	Sugar
2	Large carrots, finely grated
14oz	Tin of crushed pineapple, well drained
1 cup	Raisins (optional)
½ cup	Walnuts, chopped (optional)

Icing:

4oz	Philadelphia cheese
¼lb	Softened butter
2½ cups	Icing sugar
½ tsp	Vanilla essence

❶ Sieve together the flour, baking powder, baking soda and salt. ❷ Then in a separate bowl mix together the eggs, vegetable oil, sugar, carrots, pineapple, raisins and walnuts. ❸ Then add in dry ingredients and mix, but do not overmix. ❹ Bake at 170°C for 55 minutes in a 13x9 inch cake tin. Test centre with a toothpick to check when ready. ❺ Mix the cheese, softened butter, icing sugar and vanilla essence and ice the cake.

Rod Ferrier
Division of Cancer Sciences and Molecular Pathology,
University of Glasgow

COFFEE BUNS

16oz	Self raising flour
8oz	Sugar
1½ tsp	Coffee powder
8oz	Margarine
1	Egg
5oz	Currants

❶ Cream margarine and sugar together, beat in egg. ❷ Add coffee powder and currants. ❸ Knead in flour. ❹ Roll out into small balls and flatten. ❺ Brush with egg. ❻ Bake at Gas Mark 5 for 20 minutes.

Dorothy Holmstrom

CHOCOLATE CAKE

Makes 1 cake

150g	Self raising flour
25g	Cocoa powder
165g	Caster sugar
165g	Margarine
1 tsp	Baking powder (heaped)
3	Large eggs

Icing:

75g	Butter
150g	Icing sugar
4 tsp	Cocoa powder
2 tsp	Coffee granules

❶ Mix these ingredients together without overbeating. ❷ Divide mixture equally between 2x20cm sandwich tins. ❸ Bake at Fan 150°C. Leave to cool.
❹ Blend butter, icing sugar, cocoa powder and coffee granules with about 1 tablespoon of boiling water. Beat all the ingredients together to form a soft icing and use to fill and cover the cake.

Carol Guthrie
Glasgow

MAUREEN'S CARROT CAKE

Makes 1 cake

175g Light muscovado sugar
175 ml Sunflower oil
3 Large eggs, lightly beaten
140g Carrots, grated
100g Raisins
1 Large orange, zested
175g Self raising flour
1 tsp Bicarbonate of soda
1 tsp Ground cinnamon
Grated nutmeg

Icing:

175g Icing sugar
1½ tbsp Orange juice

Preheat the oven to 160-180°C. Oil and line the base and sides of 18cm (7 inch) square or 8 inch round cake tin with baking parchment. ❶ Put the sugar in a bowl and add oil and eggs. Lightly mix with a wooden spoon. ❷ Stir in grated carrots, raisins and orange zest. ❸ Mix flour, bicarbonate of soda and spices and sift into the bowl. Lightly mix all ingredients together. The mixture should be soft and almost runny. ❹ Pour mixture into tin and bake for 40-45 minutes until firm and springy. Cool in tin for 5 minutes. Turn out and cool on rack. (The cake can be frozen at this point). ❺ Beat together the icing sugar and orange juice until smooth – the icing should be as runny as single cream. Drizzle over the top of the cake in diagonal lines.

Maureen Dorward
Aberdeen

WILLIAM'S PANCAKES

225g **Plain flour** (or ½ white, ½ wholemeal)
2 tsp **Baking powder (level)**
2 tsp **Mixed spice (level)**
1 **Egg**
450ml **Rice milk**
1 tsp **Vanilla extract**

❶ Sift dry ingredients in a bowl. ❷ Mix liquid ingredients together thoroughly, preferably using an electric hand whisk. ❸ Combine dry and liquid ingredients. ❹ Cook pancakes in a frying pan over a fairly hot heat, turning when the bubbles begin to pop. ❺ Serve warm with maple syrup or dairy free spread and strawberry jam – a real treat!

A dairy free family favourite and I know that many women who have been affected by breast cancer try to avoid dairy products and struggle to find recipes to suit them.

ʹif using all white flour, reduce liquid amount by using 1 egg plus enough milk to equal 450ml.

Sharon Shortt
Stirling

BETTY'S CARROT CAKE

Makes 1-2 cakes

11oz	Self raising flour
1¾ tsp	Baking powder
1½ tsp	Baking soda
1¾ tsp	Cinnamon
½ tsp	Salt
4	Eggs, beaten
235g	(8oz) Granulated sugar
187ml	(8fl oz) Vegetable oil
290g	(10oz) Carrots, grated

Icing:

100g	(4oz) Philadelphia cream cheese
50g	(2oz) Butter, melted
225g	(8oz) Icing sugar, sifted
2 tsp	Vanilla flavouring
1 tsp	Lemon juice

Preheat oven to 150°C/325°F/Gas Mark 3. Grease and flour 2x8 inch sandwich tins. ❶ Sieve together flour, baking powder, baking soda, cinnamon and salt. ❷ In another bowl make sure beaten eggs are thick then gradually add all the sugar, beating continually. ❸ Gradually add all the oil. ❹ Fold in dry ingredients and carrots alternately, being careful not to overwork the mixture. ❺ Pour into prepared tins. Bake for 35 minutes or until wooden cocktail stick comes out clean. ❻ Icing: Beat cream cheese until soft and creamy. ❼ Mix together melted butter and the cream cheese. ❽ Fold in icing sugar until smooth enough for spreading. ❾ Beat in vanilla and lemon juice. If mixture seems runny refrigerate for 1 hour before use. Cakes can be sandwiched together or iced as 2 separate cakes.

Betty Brodie
Falkirk

DOUBLE DECADENCE GINGER AND ORANGE CHOCOLATE CHIP MUFFIN

Makes 12 muffins

115g	Unsalted butter, melted and cooled
2	Large eggs
180ml	Buttermilk
2 tsp	Pure vanilla extract
3 tbsp	Ginger syrup from preserved stem ginger jar
230g	Plain flour
60g	Unsweetened cocoa powder
260g	Soft light brown sugar
1 tsp	Baking powder
1 tsp	Baking soda
½ tsp	Salt
150g	Dark orange chocolate broken in to small chips (or dark chocolate chips if being less decadent!)
80-100g	Preserved stem ginger (depending on how much ginger you like), sliced and chopped into small pieces – keep a tablespoon aside to put on top of muffins before baking

Preheat oven to 190°C/Gas Mark 5. Butter or line 12 x 2¾x1½ inch muffin cups. ❶ In a large bowl whisk together the eggs, buttermilk, vanilla extract and ginger syrup. ❷ In another large bowl whisk together the flour, cocoa powder, sugar, baking powder, baking soda, and salt. Make sure there are no lumps in the sugar. ❸ Add the bulk of the chopped ginger and mix through. ❹ Stir in the orange-chocolate chips. ❺ With a rubber spatula fold the wet ingredients, along with the melted butter, into the dry ingredients. Do not over mix the batter or the muffins will be tough. It doesn't matter if it appears that all the dry mixture has not been mixed in. ❻ Spoon the mix in to the muffin cups (they will be full). ❼ Put 3-4 pieces of the preserved chopped ginger on top of each muffin. Place in centre of oven and bake for about 25-27 minutes or until skewer comes out clean and they are firm to touch. Leave to cool for about 5 minutes before removing from baking tin and leave to cool on the wire rack. Best eaten on the day of baking or keep in an airtight container for up to 2 days.

A fantastic combination of spicy ginger, contrasting with zesty dark orange chocolate in a rich chocolate muffin. Great at any time of day.

Ross McDonald

FRIENDSHIP CAKE

Makes 1-2 cakes

Day 1 **Add 1 cup each of sugar, self raising flour and milk. This is now your 'starter'**

Day 2 **Stir. Mix it well**

Day 3-4 **Leave alone – do nothing**

Day 5 **Repeat day 1 ie add 1 cup sugar, flour and milk**

Day 6 **Stir. Mix it well**

Day 7-9 **Leave**

Day 10 **Remove 3 cupfuls and pass on to friends to act as their starter along with a copy of this recipe.**

Add to remaining mixture:

1 cup	**Sugar**
2 cups	**Self raising flour**
$^2/_3$ cup	**Cooking oil**
2 tsp	**Baking powder (level)**
½ cup	**Raisins**
½ cup	**Currants**
½ cup	**Sultanas**
2 tsp	**Cinnamon**
2 tsp	**Vanilla essence**
2	**Eggs**
1	**Small tin of pineapples drained and crushed**

❶ Mix everything together well and place into a greased and lined 9 inch cake tin. ❷ Bake for approximately 1¾ hrs at 180°C/350°F/Gas Mark 4. ❸ Options – add 1 cup chopped nuts or can use mixed fruit with peel. The cake can be baked a day earlier or even 2-3 days later. Use teacups.

This is a rather unusual cake recipe, but nonetheless very delicious. The idea is that a friend gives you a 'starter', you make your own cake and pass on a 'starter' to some of your friends. If you have enough friends to keep this going a while you are truly blessed.

Do not be tempted to put the mixture in the fridge at any stage during the process, nor use a food mixer.

Put the 'starter', if you have one, into a large bowl and cover.

Shauna Brown
Falkirk

MORAG'S CARROT CAKE

Makes 1 cake

7oz	Wholemeal flour
3 tsp	Mixed spice
1 tsp	Bicarbonate of soda
6oz	Soft dark brown sugar
2	Large eggs
¼ pt	Sunflower oil
1	Orange, zested
7oz	Carrots, grated
4oz	Raisins
2oz	Coconut
2oz	Walnuts, chopped

Syrup Glaze:

1	Orange, juiced
1 tbsp	Lemon juice
3oz	Soft dark brown sugar

Oil and line a 2lb loaf tin. Preheat oven to 150°C/Gas Mark 3. ❶ In a bowl mix: flour, mixed spice and bicarbonate of soda. ❷ In a second bowl mix: sugar, eggs and oil. ❸ Mix all dry ingredients into oil mixture. ❹ Add: orange zest, carrots, raisins, coconut, nuts. ❺ Pour into tin and bake for 1¾-2 hours. ❻ Mix glaze ingredients together. ❼ When cake is baked, skewer loaf while hot and pour on glaze. Leave to cool and soak in.

This cake is made in a loaf tin rather than a tray. It doesn't have a cream cheese icing, but is deliciously moist.

Morag Miller
Killearn

TOFFEE GINGER FUDGE CUPCAKES

100g	Soft butter
100g	Light brown soft sugar
1 tsp	Ground ginger
1 tsp	Vanilla extract
25g	Golden syrup
100g	Self raising flour, sifted
2	Medium eggs, beaten

Decoration:

Pieces of fudge
(chunks cut into quarters)

Fudgy icing:

25g	Butter
50g	Light brown soft sugar (or if you only have dark, that's fine too)
2 tbsp	Single cream
100g	Icing sugar, sifted

Preheat the oven to 200°C/Gas Mark 6. Line a fairy cake tin with paper cases.
❶ Ensure all ingredients are at room temperature. Either put all the ingredients into a food processor and mix until you have a smooth batter. Or take the 'traditional' route and beat the butter and sugar together until pale and creamy. ❷ Beat in the ginger, vanilla and golden syrup until combined. ❸ Add the eggs, then gradually add a little flour at a time. ❹ Spoon into the paper cases and bake in the oven for 15-20 minutes until golden and well risen. Place on a wire rack to cool. ❺ Melt the butter and brown sugar in a small saucepan until golden brown. Be careful it doesn't burn. ❻ Gently bring to the boil then add the cream and simmer for 5 minutes. Remove from the heat and beat in the icing sugar until smooth. If the icing becomes too stiff, add a tablespoon of boiling water and beat again. ❼ Spread the icing over the cakes and decorate with chunks of fudge.

Kirsteen Young
Rowan Gallery, Helensburgh

APPLE TRAY BAKE CAKE

Makes 1 cake

- 6oz Self raising flour
- 6oz Butter or margarine
- 6oz Caster sugar
- 3 Eggs
- Few drops vanilla essence
- 1lb Eating apples
- ½ Lemon, zested
- ½ Lemon, juiced
- 3 tbsp Icing sugar

① Grease a Swiss roll tin. ② Place flour, fat, sugar, eggs, grated lemon zest and vanilla essence in a large bowl and blend with mixer until smooth and creamy. ③ Spread mixture over base of tin. ④ Peel, core and quarter the apples. ⑤ Score the rounded sides with a fork and arrange on the top of the mixture. ⑥ Bake at Fan 160-170°C for 25-35 minutes. ⑦ Mix lemon juice and icing sugar and brush over cooked warm cake.

My whole family loves this cake, it disappears very quickly!

Roisin Munn

TIR NA NOG'S SCRUMMY BANANA MUFFINS

Makes 24 muffins

300g	Sultanas
525g	Plain flour
6 tsp	Baking powder
2 tsp	Bicarbonate of soda
2 tsp	Salt
375g	Margarine
450g	Caster sugar
6	Large eggs
900g	Banana, mashed
180g	Walnuts, chopped
3 tsp	Vanilla essence

Preheat oven to 180°C. ❶ Put the flour, salt, baking powder and bicarbonate of soda in a bowl and combine well. ❷ In an extra large bowl, mix the melted butter and sugar and beat until blended. ❸ Beat in the eggs 1 at a time, then the mashed banana. ❹ Stir in the sultanas, walnuts and vanilla essence, add the flour mixture a third at a time, stirring well after each addition. ❺ Spoon the mixture into muffin cases, filling each case about ½-⅔ full. ❻ Bake in the middle of the oven for 17-20 minutes, the muffins should be well risen, check they are cooked with a skewer, it should come out clean. Let the muffins sit in the tin for 10 minutes before turning out and munching them!

Cancer has touched all the staff here at the centre in one way or another.

Oona McFarlane and Nadya Loy
Tir na nOg Holistic Centre, Baltron Station

GIPSY CREAMS

8oz Self raising flour
4oz Lard
4oz Margarine
6oz Caster sugar
2 tsp Syrup
6 tsp Boiling water
1 tsp Bicarbonate of soda
   Vanilla flavouring
2 Large breakfast cups of porridge oats

❶ Cream fat and sugar. ❷ Add syrup and boiling water, then dry ingredients. ❸ Roll into marble size balls, and slice in half. Then bake in moderate oven for about 10 minutes. ❹ Make filling – mix together butter, icing sugar and cocoa powder and use to sandwich biscuits together.

My mum (Mrs Burns) favourite family recipe

Frances Lander

LEMON DRIZZLE TRAY BAKE

Self raising flour
Caster sugar
Soft butter
Eggs
Lemon, zested and juiced
Granulated sugar

Put the flour, caster sugar, butter, eggs and lemon zest in a bowl and beat until well blended. Spread the mixture in a 12x8 inch Swiss roll tin lined with baking parchment. Bake at 180°C for 15-20 minutes or until pale golden brown.

Mix together the lemon juice and granulated sugar. Spread over the cake whilst it is still warm. Leave to cool and cut into fingers.

WELSHCAKES

1lb	Flour
1 tsp	Baking powder
	Pinch of salt
10oz	Margarine
6oz	Sugar
6oz	Sultanas
1	Egg, beaten
2 tbsp	Milk

❶ Sieve together the flour, baking powder and salt. ❷ Rub in the margarine and then add the sugar and sultanas. ❸ Make a well in the middle and add the beaten egg and some milk. Mix to make a stiff dough. Add as much milk as you need. ❹ Grease a griddle and put it on the stove to heat up. You could use a very thick-based frying pan if you don't have a griddle. ❺ Roll out the dough on a floured surface to ½ inch thick and cut into rounds. ❻ Cook on the griddle, on a steady heat, turning once, until slightly risen and cooked through. Approximately 5 minutes. They need to be cooked in batches. Cool for at least a minute before eating one! These can be frozen when fully cooled. They store well for 3 months.

Cooked on a griddle (maen), these flat fruity cakes will require your attention and the dough is very delicate, but they more than repay the time you give them. A fresh warm Welshcake has been described as being 'the closest thing to heaven'.

Rachel Murray
Powys, Wales

APPLE AND CINNAMON SCONES

6oz Self raising flour
2oz Self raising wholewheat flour
1½ tsp Baking powder
35-40 oz Milk or buttermilk
1 Egg, beaten
2oz Butter
1oz Caster sugar
1oz Demerara sugar
2 tsp Ground cinnamon
½ tsp Salt
1 Cox's apple, cubed

Preheat oven to Fan 200°C/400°F. ① In a large bowl sift together salt, cinnamon, flour and baking powder. ② Cut the butter into small chunks and using your fingers, mix until the mixture resembles coarse breadcrumbs. ③ Add the apple cubes, caster sugar and demerara sugar while stirring. ④ Make a well in the middle and pour in the beaten egg, then the milk (reserving a little egg to brush the top of the scones). Mix to a soft dough consistency. ⑤ Remove from the bowl and place on a floured board. Knead the dough until smooth and without lumps. ⑥ Roll to about 1 inch thick and cut with a 2½ inch pastry cutter and place on a greased baking tray. Brush the scones with a little egg. ⑦ Place in the preheated oven and bake for about 10-15 minutes. Or until browned. Serve warm.

Gladys Cadden

STRATHENDRICK FRUIT CAKE

¾lb	Flour
½lb	Caster sugar
½ tsp	Mixed spice
1 tsp	Baking powder (small)
½lb	Butter
¾lb	Sultanas
¾lb	Currants
4	Eggs
1	Orange, zested and juiced

❶ Rinse fruit and add to zest and juice of orange. ❷ In a separate bowl cream the butter and sugar. Add eggs and flour alternatively and lastly the fruit mixture. Mix well. ❸ Bake in a slow oven for 3 hours.

Jean Macdonald
Buchanan Castle, Drymen

CHOCOLATE BROWNIES

520g	Plain chocolate
225g	Butter
3	Large eggs
225g	Caster sugar
20ml	Coffee
75g	Self raising flour
	Pinch of salt
150g	Walnuts, chopped
5ml	Vanilla essence

❶ Grease and line 2 loaf tins. Roughly chop half the chocolate and set aside. ❷ Melt the remaining chocolate and butter in microwave for 1 minute, then mix and leave to cool. ❸ Beat the eggs, sugar and coffee together in a large bowl until smooth, then slowly beat in the cooled melted mixture. ❹ Sift the flour and salt over mixture and fold in together with walnuts, vanilla essence and chopped chocolate. ❺ Put mixture in tins at Fan 180°C/Gas Mark 5 for 40-45 minutes. Leave to cool in tins then turn out on board. Trim off the crusty edges and cut into squares. Do not overcook! They should be a gooey texture.

Stuart Burch, Head Chef
Wayfarers Restaurant, Croftamie

PINK CAKE

12	Digestive biscuits
¾ cup	Demerara sugar
6 oz	Butter
1 tbsp	Self raising flour
1	Large tin of condensed milk
2 cups	Coconut

Icing:

12 oz	Icing sugar
2 oz	Butter, melted
2 tbsp	Milk
	Pink food colouring

❶ Melt butter and add crushed biscuits, sugar and flour. ❷ Bake in Swiss roll tin for 10 minutes in a moderate oven. Mix together condensed milk and coconut and spread over base (when cool). ❸ Bake 10-15 minutes, until golden brown. ❹ Mix together icing sugar, butter, milk and food colouring and ice when cool. Leave in fridge for 2 hours then cut into squares. Freezes well!

Always reminds me of happy Young Farmer meetings round the kitchen table at Laighpark Farm, Milngavie.

Shona Kyle
Gargunnock

SHEILA'S SHORTBREAD

8oz **Salted butter**
4oz **Self raising flour**
8oz **Plain flour**
2oz **Cornflour**
3½oz **Caster sugar**

① Melt butter in pan or microwave. Grease tray with some of the melted butter. ② Place all dry ingredients in bowl and mix thoroughly. ③ Add melted butter and stir in until all the butter is absorbed and mixture is crumbly but holding together. ④ Turn into tin and smooth – then fork all over. ⑤ Pop into oven – preheated to 180°C for 15 minutes and then reduce to 140°C for another 20 minutes. ⑥ These times may vary with different ovens. Obviously fan ovens will differ and you may need to reduce heat and timing. Dredge with caster sugar and cut into pieces while still hot!!!

Enjoy!

Auntie Shiela

ABERDEEN BUTTERIES

Makes 24 pieces

3 cups	Plain flour (teacups)
2 tsp	Sugar
1oz	Yeast
1½ cups	Lukewarm water
4oz	Trex or cooking fat
1oz	Margarine
1 tsp	Salt
	Self raising flour (for board)

❶ Put the flour into a basin. Mix yeast and sugar until watery. Add to flour with the lukewarm water. ❷ Put a cloth over the basin and set in warmth for 30 minutes. ❸ Put Trex and salt on a plate and mix. ❹ Turn dough onto a floured board and knead. ❺ Spread half of the Trex onto the dough and knead. ❻ Repeat with the remainder of the Trex. ❼ Cut the dough into 24 pieces. ❽ Keeping self raising flour on the board knead the pieces until flat. Set the pieces on a baking tray for 30 minutes. ❾ Place a knob of margarine on each piece and put them in a hot oven at Gas Mark 6 for 15-20 minutes until they are brown and crisp.

Wilma Murray
Milngavie

SHORTBREAD

Makes 25-30 biscuits

- 8oz **Plain flour**
- 4oz **Cornflour**
- 4oz **Caster sugar**
- 8oz **Cheap butter**
-      **Pinch of salt**

① Sift all flour and salt together. ② Mix in butter and sugar and knead until smooth paste. ③ Roll out to ½ centimetre thick. ④ Cut into rounds or as preferred. ⑤ Bake 12-18 minutes, Gas Mark 4-6. ⑥ Sprinkle with caster sugar.

Dorothy Holmstrom

MRS PRYDE'S EMPIRE BISCUITS

175g Margarine or soft butter
 50g Icing sugar
175g Plain flour
 50g Cornflour
       Raspberry jam

Decoration:

300g Icing sugar
2 tbsp Hot (not boiling) water
       Cherries

Preheat oven to 375°F ❶ In a bowl, cream the margarine and 50g icing sugar together. ❷ Mix the plain flour and cornflour together and add to the mixture in the bowl. Mix together to make a dough. ❸ Roll out and cut into round shapes. ❹ Bake in the oven on a baking tray on the middle shelf for 15 minutes. Remove from the oven and place on a grill to cool. ❺ Once totally cooled, jam the biscuits together. ❻ Icing: Put a couple of tablespoons of hot water into a bowl. ❼ Sieve in the icing sugar and add more water if necessary, spoon onto the biscuits, once the icing starts to set, add a cherry on top.

Mrs Pryde

HOMEMADE TOASTED MUESLI

6-8 servings

300g	Rolled oats
125ml	Apple juice or pineapple juice (buy fresh if possible)
2 tbsp	Vegetable oil
80g	Hazelnuts, very roughly chopped
125g	Sunflower seeds
40g	Pumpkin seeds
40g	Sesame seeds
30g	Flaked coconut
100g	Dried fruits eg cranberries, blueberries, apricots, sultanas (optional)

Preheat the oven to 160°C/315°F/Gas Mark 2-3. ❶ Place all the ingredients except the hazelnuts in a bowl and stir well to combine. ❷ Spread the mixture evenly over a large baking tray and place in the oven for 15 minutes stirring occasionally. ❸ After 15 minutes add the hazelnuts to the baking tray and cook for a further 15-20 minutes, stirring occasionally. ❹ Remove from the oven and leave to cool. ❺ Once cool add your selection of dried fruits. Store the muesli in an airtight container – it will keep for up to a month. Serve with yoghurt and fresh fruit such as blueberries, raspberries or nectarines.

Jacqui Crawford
Glasgow

DESSERTS

MUM'S TRUFFLES

Makes 30

20	Digestive biscuits, crushed
1	Tin of condensed milk
8oz	Butter or margarine
10 tbsp	Desiccated coconut
10 tbsp	Drinking chocolate
	Vermicelli to coat

❶ Melt butter in a pan, add all ingredients and mix well. ❷ Roll a spoonful of mixture by hand into balls and coat with vermicelli or desiccated coconut.

They don't last long enough to keep in the fridge!

Katie Murray
London

PEPPERMINT CREAMS

Makes 20

1 Egg white
1 tsp Oil of Peppermint
10-12oz Icing sugar, sifted

❶ Beat egg white until fluffy and then add oil of peppermint. ❷ Gradually stir in icing sugar, adding sufficient to form a very stiff mixture. ❸ Turn mixture onto surface, thickly dusted with sifted icing sugar and roll out to ¼ inch thick. Cut into rounds with a 1 inch cutter. Gather trimmings together and knead lightly and re-roll. Re-cut until all of the mixture is used up. ❹ Leave for about one day for creams to become firm and set.

Lynn Murray
Buchanan Castle, Drymen

TABLET

1 **Pack of unsalted Lurpak butter**
2lb **Caster sugar**
1 cup **Full fat milk**
1 **Tin of condensed milk**

❶ Slowly melt the Lurpak, then add the sugar and milk. ❷ Boil gently for about 20-25 minutes, you will notice the texture changing, becoming much thicker. Stir occasionally. ❸ After 20-25 minutes add 1 tin of condensed milk, boil gently (not too vigorously) for a further 25-30 minutes. The colour will deepen and mixture thicken. The test for readiness is a cold cup of water, drop a little tablet into the water and if it forms a gluey substantial ball – it's ready. Remove from heat. ❹ Now take the hand held mixer and beat/whisk on full (max) for 10 minutes until the mixture is very thick but you can still transfer into a flat dish, or baking tray. I use a very flat Pyrex dish (buttered). Leave to cool, cut into squares and enjoy!

Caroline Clark
Dyrion

MASCARPONE TABLET

75g	(3oz) Butter
8oz	Tub mascarpone cheese
500g	Golden caster sugar
½ tsp	Vanilla extract

❶ Place a heavy-based pan on the lowest heat on the cooker. ❷ Put butter and mascarpone in a pan and slowly melt, stirring occasionally. ❸ Stir in the sugar and leave on the lowest heat – stir mixture regularly as it may start to burn. Leave on lowest heat for about 50 minutes – mixture will start to bubble; do not be tempted to turn up the heat! Mixture will go slightly darker after bubbling for a while – remember to stir now and again. ❹ Add vanilla essence just before taking off the heat. ❺ Beat mixture for about 4-6 minutes until it starts to thicken and your arm gets tired! ❻ Pour into a non-stick baking paper lined tray and leave to cool. Cut into bite-sized pieces before tablet sets or it will just crack.

Enjoy!!!

Ruth Tainton
Edinburgh

CHOCOLATE PISTACHIO FUDGE

350g	Dark chocolate, at least 70% cocoa solids, chopped
1 x 397g	Tin of condensed milk
30g	Butter
	Pinch of salt
150g	Unsalted pistachios, shells removed (But you can make it without the pistachios)

❶ Place the chopped chocolate, condensed milk, butter and salt into a heavy-based pan over a low heat and stir until melted and well combined. ❷ Place the nuts into a freezer bag and bash them with a rolling pin, until broken up into large and small pieces. ❸ Add the nuts to the chocolate mixture and stir well. ❹ Pour the mixture into a 23cm square tray, smoothing the top with a wet palette knife. ❺ Let the fudge cool, then refrigerate until set. ❻ Cut into small pieces approximately 3x2cm. ❼ Once cut, the fudge can be kept in the freezer – there's no need to thaw, just eat straight away.

Heather Hodgson
Buchanan Castle, Drymen

CHOCOLATE TRUFFLES

4oz	Butter
8oz	Icing sugar
2oz	Ground almonds
4oz	Coconut
4 tsp	Strong black coffee
4oz	Chocolate, melted

❶ Combine all ingredients together in a food mixer and chill for 2 hours.
❷ Make teaspoon size pieces and roll into balls. ❸ Coat in melted chocolate.
Using 2 forks, drop into truffle cases. Decorate, if desired, with chopped
nuts, chocolate vermicelli, etc.

Joan Reece
Drymen

JANIE'S TABLET

2lb Caster sugar
1 Large tin of condensed milk
1 cup Water
4oz Butter

❶ Melt butter and water in a large pan. ❷ Add sugar gradually, then add condensed milk. ❸ Bring to the boil slowly, stirring constantly, and boil for about 15 minutes, to soft ball stage. ❹ Remove from heat and beat thoroughly until 'sugary'. ❺ Pour into greased tin, mark with a knife when cool.

Wendi Bates
Balfron

CHOCOLATE MINT BAR

8oz Digestive biscuits, crushed
4oz Peppermint creams, chopped
1 Egg, beaten
4oz Margarine
4oz Caster sugar
2 tbsp Drinking chocolate
8oz Chocolate

❶ Melt margarine and sugar then add drinking chocolate, egg, biscuits and peppermint creams. ❷ Press into swiss roll tin. ❸ Allow to harden. ❹ Cover with melted chocolate. When set cut into fingers.

Heather Hodgson
Buchanan Castle, Drymen

SHORTCRUST PASTRY APPLE PIE

Makes 1 pie

8oz	Self raising flour
2oz	Margarine
2oz	Trex cooking fat
	Pinch of salt
2 dsp	Granulated sugar
½ mug	Cold water
1½lb	Cooking apples
2oz	Granulated sugar
2oz	Soft brown sugar
	Caster sugar for dusting

❶ Stew apples in a little water with 2oz of granulated sugar and soft brown sugar until soft, but not mushy. ❷ Rub fat into flour to make fine breadcrumbs, and add 2 dessert spoons of sugar and enough water to make a stiff dough. ❸ Knead lightly for a few seconds – do not over-handle. ❹ Wrap in cling film and chill in the fridge for about 30 minutes. ❺ Roll out half the dough and use to line a greased pie dish. Prick all over the base with a fork. ❻ Put apples in the base and cover with the other half of rolled out dough. ❼ Make 1-2 vents to allow the steam to come out and brush the top with some milk. ❽ Put pie in oven at 180°C for 40-45 minutes until golden brown. Dust top with caster sugar.

Doreen Haddow
Buchanan Castle, Drymen

LEMON MERINGUE PIE

Makes 1 pie

- 2oz **Butter**
- 6oz **Digestive biscuits, crushed**
- 1 **Tin of condensed milk**
- 2 **Eggs, separated**
- 2 **Lemons**
- 4oz **Caster sugar**

❶ Melt butter, stir in crushed biscuits and press mixture into flan dish.
❷ Beat together condensed milk, egg yolks, grated lemon zest and juice
and pour over biscuit base. ❸ Whisk egg whites until stiff, stir in caster sugar
gradually and cover pie with this mixture. ❹ Bake for 15-20 minutes at 190°C.

Wendi Bates
Bolton

PINK PAVLOVA

4	Egg whites
250g	Caster sugar
1½ tsp	Cornflour
1½ tsp	White wine vinegar
375ml	Double cream
	Punnet of raspberries
	or strawberries

Preheat oven to 160°C/325°F/Gas Mark 3. Mark a 9 inch circle on a piece of non-stick baking paper, turn the paper over and line a baking tray with it. ❶ Whisk the egg whites until stiff, then add the sugar, 1 teaspoon at a time, whisking the mixture constantly. ❷ Blend the cornflour and vinegar and whisk into the egg white mixture. ❸ Spread the mixture inside the circle on the baking paper, building up the sides so they are higher than the middle. ❹ Place in the oven immediately reducing the heat to 150°C/300°F/Gas Mark 2. Bake the meringue for 1 hour then turn off oven, leaving meringue inside. ❺ Peel paper off meringue, place on a plate and leave to cool. Whip double cream until stiff then stir in ¾ of the raspberries or strawberries (chopped). Use the remaining fruit to decorate.

Jean Nicholson

LEMON SYLLABUB

Serves 8

4 **Egg whites**
½ pt **Not too dry white wine**
8oz **(125g) Caster sugar**
1 pt **Double cream**
1 **Lemon, juiced**
Crystallised angelica

① Whisk egg whites in a large bowl until quite firm. ② Sieve and gradually fold the caster sugar into the egg whites. ③ Fold in the lemon juice followed by the wine. ④ Complete by folding in the not too stiffly whipped cream. ⑤ Immediately ladle it into tall wine glasses, being careful to keep mixture well folded. ⑥ Decorate each glass with a small piece of angelica. Leave to separate into a delicious cream to be eaten with a spoon, and, underneath, a wine whey to be finally drunk.

This syllabub should be made at least 3 hours before it is served.

Margaret Robertson

NON COOKED CHEESECAKE

14-16 **Digestive biscuits**
3oz **Butter**
½ **Tin of condensed milk**
1/3 cup **Lemon juice**
200g **Philadelphia cheese**

① Crush biscuits in a food processor. Melt butter and mix with the crushed biscuits. Press into flan tray. ② In food processor, mix condensed milk, lemon juice and Philadelphia cheese. Pour over biscuit base and chill. ③ Serve with chocolate curls or any fruit of your choice.

Very easy – Got this from my Ma-in-law. It has helped feed her son for many years!!!

Angela Mackenzie

FREDA'S STICKY TOFFEE PUDDING

4oz	Butter
8oz	Self raising flour
3	Eggs, beaten
6oz	Caster sugar
8oz	Dates, chopped
½ pt	Boiling water
1 tsp	Bicarbonate of soda
1 tsp	Vanilla essence

Sauce:

4oz	Butter
8oz	Soft brown sugar
½ pt	Double cream

❶ Pour boiling water over dates, vanilla essence and bicarbonate of soda.
❷ Cream butter and sugar together until light and fluffy. Slowly add beaten eggs, mixing well after each addition. ❸ Fold in flour. ❹ Combine the 2 mixtures, folding gently (the mixture looks very sloppy but is supposed to). ❺ Pour into a 14x9 inch tin and bake in a preheated oven at 150°C/300°F for 45 minutes, until cooked through and springy to the touch. ❻ Sauce: Place all the ingredients in a saucepan and heat gently until butter has melted and sugar has dissolved, increase the heat and bring to the boil, stirring continuously. ❼ Boil for 3 minutes and then pour over sponge mixture. Serve hot or cold with cream or ice cream.

This has to be the best sticky toffee pudding I have ever tasted. It is my mum in law's recipe.

Freda Robertson
Buchanan Castle, Drymen

HOT CHOCOLATE FUDGE BROWNIE PUDDING

Serves 4

125g	Plain flour
2 tsp	Baking powder (level)
25g	Cocoa powder
150g	Golden caster sugar
200ml	Crème fraîche
50g	Unsalted butter, melted and slightly cooled
50g	Pecan nuts, chopped into large pieces
1 tsp	Vanilla extract
	Salt

Chocolate fudge sauce:

50g	Good quality plain chocolate, roughly chopped
110g	Dark muscovado sugar
25g	Cocoa powder, sifted
2 tsp	Vanilla extract
310ml	Cold water

Preheat oven to 170°C/325°F/Gas Mark 3. ❶ Place all the sauce ingredients in a saucepan, and bring slowly to the boil, stirring occasionally. ❷ Boil for 2-3 minutes, stirring constantly, then remove from the heat and leave to cool for at least 15 minutes. ❸ For the brownie pudding, sift the flour, baking powder, cocoa, sugar and a pinch of salt into a bowl and mix together. ❹ Add crème fraîche, melted butter, pecans and vanilla extract and stir together. ❺ Spoon the mixture into a 1½ litre (2½ pint) baking dish about 5cm (2 inch) deep. ❻ Level the surface and pour over the sauce and immediately place in the oven for 40-45 minutes. The brownie will rise to the surface and feel spongy. Leave to cool for 5-10 minutes and serve warm with vanilla ice cream or cream.

Sharmi Musgrave
Buchanan Castle, Drymen

STRAWBERRY CHEESE GATEAU

8oz	Cream cheese
4 tbsp	Caster sugar (level)
1	Orange, zested
1 tbsp	Brandy or orange liqueur (I use more!)
½ pt	Double cream
16	Sponge fingers
2 tbsp	Strawberry jam (level)
½lb	Strawberries
	Greaseproof paper
	Little cooking oil

❶ Cut pieces of greaseproof paper to fit the base and sides of a 2lb loaf tin. Brush inside of tin with oil and press greaseproof paper into position. ❷ Put cream cheese and caster sugar into a bowl and mix thoroughly. ❸ Add grated orange zest, liqueur and double cream and continue mixing until it thickens. ❹ Put a third of mixture into tin and smooth over the surface. Cover with sponge fingers. ❺ Beat jam with fork and spread half of it thinly over sponge fingers. ❻ Cut strawberries in half and cover sponge fingers. Continue in same way using another third of cream mixture, the remaining sponge fingers and jam and the rest of the strawberries. Finish with the remaining cream mixture and smooth over surface. You can freeze at this stage if you wish or leave gateau in the fridge overnight or for at least 2 hours. ❼ Run knife round the top edge of the gateau to release it then turn it on to a plate. Peel off paper and garnish with strawberries. If your gateau is frozen make sure to defrost for at least 4 hours in the fridge.

It is really easy to make, you can freeze it and take it out the day you want to use it, but most of all it looks great and tastes delicious.

Loretta Murray
Bearsden

AFTER EIGHT CHEESECAKE

75g Margarine
175g Digestive biscuits, crushed
2-3 tbsp Drinking chocolate
225g Cream cheese
200g Caster sugar
200ml Whipping cream
½ tsp Vanilla essence
100g After Eight mints
1 tbsp Water
After Eights/Mint Aero
to decorate

❶ Melt margarine, add digestive biscuits and drinking chocolate. Mix well together and press into tin. ❷ Place cream cheese, caster sugar, whipping cream and vanilla essence in a bowl. Mix on a high speed until thickened. ❸ Spread evenly on top of biscuit base. ❹ Melt After Eights and water together. Pour onto cheesecake, spread on top and leave until it has set. Decorate with grated Mint Aero and cream.

This is the recipe for my favourite dessert – After Eight Cheesecake. It's fairly straight-forward, full of calories (aren't all the best recipes!!!) and always a winner. Who doesn't love After Eights, and who doesn't love cheesecake – a winning combination!!!

Fiona Ingram
Elderslie

WHITE CHOCOLATE
ICE CREAM

Medium eggs
Caster sugar
White chocolate
Double cream

Whisk sugar and eggs until light and 'fluffy'. Melt white chocolate and add to lightly whipped cream. Mix all ingredients together until well mixed and blended together. Pour into a loaf tin lined with cling film and place in freezer for minimum of 4 hours.

Lovely served over warm apple crumble...

Enjoy!!! And forget the calories!!!

VANILLA PANNA COTTA WITH BLACKBERRY SAUCE

Serves 8-10

6	Gelatine leaves
500ml	Double cream
500ml	Full cream milk
2	Vanilla pods, split lengthways and seeds scraped out
50g	Caster sugar

Blackberry sauce:

300g	Blackberries
75g	Caster sugar
1-2 tbsp	Water (if needed)
	Splash of cassis (optional)
	Mint leaves (for decorating)
	Icing sugar (for dusting)

❶ Place the gelatine leaves in a bowl of cold water for 10 minutes until soft.
❷ Place the milk, cream, vanilla pods and seeds and sugar into a pan and bring to a simmer. Remove the vanilla pods. ❸ Squeeze the water out of the gelatine leaves, add to the pan and take off the heat. Stir until the gelatine has dissolved. ❹ Pour the mixture into 1 large ring mould/jelly mould or divide into individual moulds and leave to cool. Place in fridge for several hours, until set. ❺ For the sauce, place the sugar, berries and cassis (if using) into a small pan and bring to the boil. Reduce the heat and simmer until the sugar has dissolved. Add 1-2 tablespoons of water if sugar starts to caramelise. Allow to cool. ❻ To serve, run a blunt knife around the edge of the mould and turn out onto a plate. (If the panna cotta does not come out of the mould, hold for a few seconds in a bowl of hot water and then turn out). Spoon the sauce around or serve separately. Garnish with mint leaves and dust with icing sugar.

Sharmi Musgrave
Buchanan Castle, Drymen

WHITE GRAPE AND GINGER SYLLABUB

2 lb	Seedless grapes
8 oz	Ginger biscuits, crushed
4	Egg whites, stiffly beaten
10fl oz	White wine
6 oz	Caster sugar
15fl oz	Double cream
1 tsp	Ground ginger or to taste
	A generous squirt of lemon juice

❶ Arrange the grapes in layers on the dishes. ❷ Beat egg whites and cream in separate bowls and have a third large bowl to hand. (I use a bowl with about a 10 inch diameter) ❸ Add the sugar to the beaten egg whites. ❹ Pour wine and lemon juice over egg whites and mix in gently. ❺ Combine whites and cream in the bigger bowl. ❻ Pour gently over the grapes/biscuits and chill preferably overnight. ❼ Overfill the dishes because the mixture 'shrinks' as the wine seeps into the gingered biscuits.

Laura E. Alexander
West Kilbride

APPLE AND MARSHMALLOW BAKE

Bramley apples
Sugar
Marshmallows

❶ Stew Bramley apples with sugar until soft. ❷ Put into shallow ovenproof dish. ❸ Cut marshmallows in half with scissors. ❹ Arrange marshmallows, close together, on top of the apples. ❺ Put in microwave for 1-2 minutes on high, until marshmallows are melted.

Serve either hot or cold.

Wilma Snoddy

PEAR BELLE HELENE

Serves 4

1 tsp	Vanilla essence
3 tbsp	Granulated sugar
4	Pears (ripe but still firm)
1½ litres	Cold water

Chocolate Sauce:

100g	Continental plain chocolate
1 tbsp	Butter
3 tbsp	Golden syrup
4 tbsp	Milk

❶ Pour 1½ litres of cold water into a pan, add vanilla essence and sugar. Stir well and bring to the boil. Simmer for 1-2 minutes. ❷ Peel pears, leaving stalk intact and cut a sliver from the base to allow the pears to stand up in the pan. ❸ Place the pears in the liquid, adding a little more if needed to ensure the pears are fully submerged. Cover with a lid and simmer 10-15 minutes, depending on ripeness of pears. ❹ Test pears are tender by piercing with the tip of a sharp knife. Drain well and discard the poaching liquid. ❺ When pears have cooled a little, remove the cores using an apple corer. ❻ Make the sauce by placing all ingredients in a small pan and melt slowly over gentle heat. Stir occasionally until all melted and glossy.

Serve the pears warm with the chocolate sauce and ice cream.

Terri O'Neill
Berkhamstead

BRANDY SWEET DREAM

2	Packets of marshmallows
2 tbsp	Instant coffee
½ pt	Boiling water
5 tbsp	Brandy
½ pt	Whipped cream
1	Chocolate flake

❶ Put marshmallows, coffee, boiling water and brandy in a liquidiser. ❷ Blend well then pour into a glass bowl and allow to cool. ❸ Place in fridge to set. Serve decorated with whipped cream and a flake.

Aileen Stewart (as passed down from her mother)
Dunblane

THINK PINK RASPBERRY CHARLOTTE

1 lb	Raspberries (keep a few aside for decoration)
4oz	Sugar
½ pt	Water
2 dsp	Cornflour (level)
2	Eggs
3 tbsp	Double cream
	Few drops of lemon juice
1	Packet of sponge fingers
4oz	Icing sugar

❶ Melt sugar and water in a pan over a low heat then add raspberries and cook over a very low heat until tender, but still whole (5-6 minutes). ❷ Drain syrup into a measuring jug and set the raspberries aside. ❸ Put the cornflour into a small pan and gradually blend in ½ pint of the raspberry syrup. Keep the rest for the meringue. Cook over a low heat, stirring constantly until the mixture is clear and beginning to thicken. Remove from heat. ❹ Separate the eggs. Beat together yolks and cream and add this to the syrup mixture. Add lemon juice. ❺ Cut 1 rounded end off each of the sponge fingers. Put a ½ inch layer of raspberry cream in the base of a 1 pint soufflé dish. ❻ Stand sponge fingers, cut side downwards, closely round the inside of the dish – they need to stand about 1 inch above the rim. Alternate layers of fruit and cream finishing with cream. ❼ For meringue topping, put egg whites, icing sugar and 3 tablespoons of raspberry juice in a basin over a saucepan of simmering water and whisk steadily until mixture stands in soft peaks. Remove basin from heat and continue whisking until meringue is cool. Pile this on top of the raspberry cream. ❽ Bake the charlotte at the bottom of a low oven at 160°C/Fan 140°C for 30 minutes or until meringue is lightly coloured. Serve cold decorated with raspberries.

Christine Gastall
Drymen

CHERRY TRIFLE

4	Chocolate chip muffins
2	Tins of black cherries in heavy syrup
1	Jelly (black cherry or blackcurrant)
	Kirsch liqueur
10fl oz	Whipping cream
1	Tub mascarpone cheese
	Chocolate chips

❶ Cut the muffins in quarters and place in the bottom of a trifle bowl. Place cherries on top. ❷ Melt jelly in microwave for a few seconds with a little water to dissolve and then make up the liquid with juice from tinned cherries. ❸ Pour over the sponge and add some Kirsch. Allow to set in fridge. ❹ When chilled, mix the whipped cream with the mascarpone cheese and use to top the dessert. Decorate with chocolate chips.

Quick to make and tastes really luxurious.

Rhona Baxter
Aberdeen

CHOCOLATE ESPRESSO TORTE

350g	Dark chocolate, melted
350g	Unsalted butter, melted
175g	Granulated sugar
175ml	Strong coffee (espresso is best)
5	Eggs

Ganache for glazing:

375g	Dark chocolate, melted
185ml	Cream, boiled
12.5g	Glucose

❶ Use a small pot half filled with water and with a bowl over to melt the chocolate. ❷ Melt the butter in a saucepan over a low heat. ❸ Combining the sugar and eggs – whisk just until eggs are broken and mixture is blended. ❹ Pour individually the coffee, butter and chocolate slowly while stirring. ❺ A cake ring is best. Wrap aluminum foil tightly around the bottom with the shiny side up. Place the ring on a baking tray. ❻ The torte is baked when it is springy to the touch. Once cooled to room temperature, take a small knife and loosen from the cake ring. Place in fridge for at least 4 hours, and ideally overnight. For ganache add hot cream to the chocolate and stir until smooth. Add glucose, stir until smooth. Glaze torte while ganache is warm. Enjoy.

This wonderful gluten free recipe was invented by a chef friend. He assures me it is easy – and I can vouch for it tasting scrummy.

Moira Gourlay
Ontario, Canada

CRANACHAN

1oz Medium oatmeal
2 tbsp Whisky
2oz Caster sugar
1lb Frozen forest fruits
(or mixture of summer
and forest fruits)
8oz Mascarpone cheese
½ pt Whipping cream
3 tbsp Clear honey
1oz Hazelnuts, toasted
and chopped

❶ Soak the oatmeal in whisky for 2 hours. ❷ Sprinkle caster sugar over the thawed fruit. ❸ Cover and leave while the oatmeal is soaking. ❹ Blend the cheese together with the oatmeal mixture. ❺ Whip the cream until it forms soft peaks. ❻ Fold the cream and honey into the oatmeal mixture. ❼ Put the fruit into a large serving dish. ❽ Cover with the cream and oatmeal mixture (making swirls). ❾ Top with toasted hazelnuts.

Val Sneddon
Falkirk

STRAWBERRY AND PASSION FRUIT MERINGUE

4 **Egg whites**
200g **Caster sugar**
200g **Lemon curd**
3 **Passion fruit, strain seeds and keep both seeds and juice**
150ml **Double cream**
10 **Strawberries, chopped**

Line a 23x30cm swiss roll tin with baking paper. ❶ Whisk egg whites. ❷ Slowly add sugar until stiff and glossy. ❸ Spoon mixture onto baking tray and bake for 15 minutes, oven 180°C, until crisp on the outside. Allow to cool completely. ❹ Lay a fresh piece of greaseproof paper out and flip the meringue over onto it. Carefully pull away the used paper. ❺ Spread lemon curd over it and then the passion fruit seeds. ❻ Whip cream with passion fruit juice and spread on top of the curd. Sprinkle strawberries over. ❼ Roll the meringue lengthways. Dust with icing sugar to serve.

Paula Guy
Killearn

LEMON FREEZE

2oz	Cornflake crumbs or crushed whole cornflakes
3oz	Caster sugar
2oz	Butter, melted
2	Eggs, separated
1	Small tin of condensed milk
¼ pt	Double cream
2	Lemons, finely zested and juiced

① Measure the crumbs into a basin; add 2oz of the sugar. Using a fork, stir in the melted butter. ② Reserve 2 tablespoons of the mixture and pat the remainder firmly over the base of a large refrigerator ice tray. ③ To make the dessert easier to remove after freezing, first line the tray with a strip of kitchen foil so that the foil runs along the base and overlaps each end of the tray. ④ Set aside to chill while preparing the lemon filling. ⑤ Mix the egg yolks, condensed milk and cream in a mixing basin. ⑥ Add the finely grated zest and strained lemon juice, and stir until the mixture thickens. ⑦ Beat the egg whites until stiff; whisk in the remaining sugar. Fold the beaten egg whites into the lemon mixture and pour into the prepared tray. ⑧ Sprinkle the reserved crumb mixture on top and freeze for 3-4 hours, or until quite firm. ⑨ To serve, loosen the sides, then, using the foil, lift out the dessert and cut into (large) portions.

This recipe was kindly given to me by my mother-in-law, Margie Fraser and recreated each Christmas by me to provide a favourite Fraser family treat.

Susan Fraser

FANTASTIC BLACK CHERRY CHEESECAKE

1 cup	Caster sugar
1	Large tub of Philadelphia cream cheese
1	Packet of Dream Topping
	Knob of butter
12	Digestives
	Fruit

❶ Mix caster sugar with Philadelphia cream cheese (you could use low fat, but hey-hoh). ❷ Make up 1 packet of Dream Topping and fold into your cheese/sugar creamy mix. ❸ Melt a knob of butter in a pan and add a dozen or so broken digestive biscuits. ❹ Push the biscuit mix into a serving dish to make the cheesecake base, add the creamy topping and then fruit of your choosing. The tins of black cherries in syrup are always good for this.

Clare Young
Buchanan Castle, Drymen

VERY EASY DELICIOUS LEMON CHEESECAKE

Serves 6

3oz	Butter, melted
5oz	Digestive biscuits, crushed
1	Lemon jelly
1	Lemon, finely zested and juiced
6oz	Cream cheese
1	Large tin of chilled evaporated milk
10oz	Tin of mandarin oranges, drained
3 tbsp	Marmalade, sieved

① Mix together the butter and biscuit crumbs and press into a greased 8 inch loose bottomed tin. ② Dissolve the jelly in ¼ pint boiling water. Mix jelly with the lemon zest, juice and cream cheese. Whisk until smooth. ③ Add the evaporated milk and whisk again. ④ Pour the mixture over the biscuit base and chill until set. ⑤ Place cheesecake on a serving plate, decorate with mandarin oranges and brush with marmalade.

Ann Graham

BEST STICKY TOFFEE PUDDING

4oz Butter, softened
6oz Caster sugar
3 Eggs, beaten
8oz Self raising flour
8oz Stoned dates, chopped
and covered with ½ pint
boiling water
1 tsp Bicarbonate of soda
1 tsp Vanilla essence
1 tbsp Coffee essence (Camp)

Toffee sauce:

½ pt Cream
8oz Butter
8oz Brown sugar

Preheat oven to 170°C. ❶ Cream butter and sugar. Slowly add eggs and fold in flour. ❷ Mix dates in water with vanilla, bicarbonate of soda and Camp coffee. ❸ Mix dates etc with cake mixture, fold carefully. ❹ Place in a 9 inch buttered tin and bake for 50-60 minutes. ❺ Put all ingredients for the toffee sauce in a saucepan and dissolve over gentle heat. Then boil quickly for 5 minutes, keep warm until ready to serve.

Marianne Ross
Drymen

5 MINUTE CHOCOLATE MUG PUDDING

Serves 2

4 tsp Flour
4 tsp Sugar
2 tsp Cocoa
1 Egg
3 tsp Milk
3 tsp Oil
3 tsp Chocolate chips (optional)
A small splash of
vanilla extract
1 Large coffee mug

❶ Add dry ingredients to mug, and mix well. ❷ Add the egg and mix thoroughly. ❸ Pour in the milk and oil and mix well. ❹ Add the chocolate chips (if using) and vanilla extract, and mix again. ❺ Put your mug in the microwave and cook for 3 minutes at 1000 watts (high). The pudding will rise over the top of the mug, but don't be alarmed! Allow to cool a little, and tip out onto a plate if desired. Eat!

The most dangerous pudding recipe. Thought you girls would like this...

And why is this the most dangerous pudding recipe in the world? Because now we are all only 5 minutes away from chocolate cake at any time of the day or night!

Heather Fair
Lisburn

EASY LEMON DESSERT

225g   Gingernuts, crushed
100g   Butter
250ml Whipping cream,
       lightly whipped
405g   Tin of sweetened
       condensed milk
    2 Lemons, finely zested
       and juiced (or 5 tbsp
       lemon juice)
       Keep a few slices of lemon
       for decoration, if desired

❶ Gently melt the butter, in a microwave, or over a low heat, and add the crushed gingernuts. Mix well. Press the mixture firmly into the base of the greased pie tin. ❷ Beat the condensed milk together with half the beaten cream and the lemon zest. Continuing to beat, add the lemon juice. The mix will thicken up. ❸ Pour over the gingernut base. Decorate with the lemon slices. ❹ Serve with the remaining whipped cream.

My mum used to make this with the cream from the top of a bottle of milk, which made it easy to make from the kitchen cupboard. We now use semi-skimmed at home, so it is better to use whipping cream. You can substitute 4 limes for the 2 lemons.

Heather Fair

ANY FLAVOUR CHEESECAKE

1 Small packet of digestive
  biscuits
4oz Butter, melted
2 Packs of low fat
  cream cheese
1 Pot Elmlea double cream
1 Pack of jelly of your choice
  made up to ¼ pint

❶ Crumble the biscuits until quite fine. ❷ Add the butter and mix well until combined. ❸ Grease a flan dish well and press the biscuit base into the dish to cover the bottom. ❹ Put all the topping ingredients (cream cheese, double cream and jelly into a liquidiser or mixing bowl and blend well. ❺ Pour topping over the base and put in the fridge to set approximately 2-3 hours. ❻ Decorate if desired.

Angela Conboy
Glasgow

PINEAPPLE DELIGHT

½lb Digestive biscuits
1 Tin of crushed pineapple
6oz Margarine or butter
4oz Icing sugar
1 Small egg
1 Carton cream

① Crumble biscuits (keep 1 out). ② Mix with 3oz melted margarine or butter and spread in flan dish. ③ Beat remaining butter or margarine, icing sugar and egg and spread over the biscuits. ④ Allow to become firm then cover with drained pineapple. ⑤ Cover with whipped cream and crumbled biscuit. Put in fridge until ready to serve.

It is good.

Bev Reid
Buchanan Castle, Drymen

WHITE CHOCOLATE AND LIME CHEESECAKE

100g Ginger nut biscuits
40g Unsalted butter
1 Lime
100g Low fat cream cheese
20g Caster sugar
150ml Double cream
75g White chocolate
(suitable for cooking)

❶ Crush the biscuits. Melt butter and mix into the biscuits. Press the mixture into a 15 inch loose bottom flan ring and chill. ❷ Wash lime, grate zest and squeeze out the juice. Set aside. ❸ Beat cream cheese and sugar together. ❹ Whisk double cream until it is standing in soft peaks. ❺ Melt chocolate and mix with cream cheese. ❻ Add lime zest and 15ml juice to the cream mixture and mix in. ❼ Fold in half of the whipped cream to the cream cheese mixture. Reserve remaining cream for piping. ❽ Spoon the cream cheese mixture over the biscuit base and chill until firm. Remove flan ring and place on a cold plate. Pipe with the remaining cream and decorate appropriately.

Elizabeth Harbison
Coleraine N. Ireland

MERINGUES

3   **Large egg whites**
3oz **Granulated sugar**
3oz **Caster sugar**
    Pinch of salt
    Whipped cream for filling

Preheat the oven to Fan 100°C/225°F. Grease a baking sheet. Add pinch of salt to the egg whites and whisk until stiff. Whisk in the granulated sugar, then fold the caster sugar into the mixture with a large metal spoon a little at a time. Either pipe the mixture or use 2 dessert spoons to shape the meringues. Place in the oven for 3 hours, then turn oven off, and leave in the oven as long as possible to dry out completely. (Overnight is ideal). For a large batch double the ingredients.

CHOCOLATE MIELIE MEAL PUDDING

Makes 25-30 Dariole moulds

20 Eggs
20 Egg yolks
500g Caster sugar
1kg Dark cooking chocolate, chopped
1kg Unsalted butter, cut into cubes
80g Mielie Meal, ground in a pestle mortar
Pinch of salt
120g Plain flour

❶ Melt the chocolate and butter over a double boiler on a low heat stirring occasionally with a spatula. ❷ Mix the eggs, egg yolks and caster sugar, until the sugar is almost dissolved. ❸ While the chocolate is melting spray the Dariole moulds with wax spray and then turn them over onto a cloth to catch the excess grease. ❹ When the chocolate mix is melted, stir slowly into the egg mixture. ❺ Mix the ground Mielie Meal, flour and salt. ❻ Whisk the Mielie Meal, flour and salt into the chocolate mixture gradually (you don't have to use all the flour mix). ❼ Fill the moulds ¾ full with the chocolate mixture. ❽ Bake at 200°C until just firm on top (approximately 7 minutes) the centre of the pudding will be liquid.

Pete Gottgens
Ardeonaig Hotel, Perthshire

EASY TWICE BAKED CHEESECAKE

		Filling:	
4oz	Self raising flour		
2oz	Caster sugar	2 x 300g	Philadelphia cream cheese
1 tsp	Lemon, zested	4oz	Caster sugar
½ tsp	Vanilla essence	1½ tsp	Self raising flour
1	Egg yolk	1½ tsp	Lemon juice
2oz	Butter	1½ tsp	Vanilla essence
		3	Eggs
		1	Egg yolk
		2 tbsp	Double cream

Preheat the oven to 180°C. Use a 9x2 inch spring form tin. ❶ Rub butter into flour, add other ingredients until blended. Press into base of tin. Prick with a fork. Bake for approximately 20 minutes until light brown. ❷ Beat cheese until creamy and smooth. ❸ Beat in sugar, a few tablespoons at a time. ❹ Sieve flour to prevent lumps. Add lemon, beaten eggs, yolk and cream. ❺ Pour on top of base and bake until dark brown, approximately 10-15 minutes in an oven at 220°C. Cake should start to rise slightly. Cool for 30 minutes. ❻ Set oven to 170°C. Return to oven for final baking to set the cake – approximately 20-30 minutes. When cake is bouncy and slightly raised in middle, like quiche it is ready. Add fruit on top if desired.

Jane Crawford
Killearn

PINK CHEESECAKE

200g	Digestive biscuits
150g	Butter
3dl	Cream
200g	Plain cream cheese
1	Package raspberry jelly (125g jelly powder)
2½dl	Water

❶ In a plastic bag, crush the digestive biscuits with a rolling pin. ❷ After the biscuits are well crushed, gradually rub in the butter. ❸ Press the crushed biscuit and butter 'dough' into an even layer in a deep pie dish, greased with butter. Set aside. ❹ Dissolve the raspberry jelly in the boiling water and allow to cool. ❺ In a bowl, combine the cream cheese and cream, mix until smooth. ❻ Add the jelly to the cheese and cream mixture and mix well. ❼ Pour the cheese, cream and jelly mix over the biscuit base. ❽ Place in the fridge and leave until set. ❾ Sometimes before the cheesecake is set, I swirl in some puréed raspberries. It looks great, and adds flavour.

Meg Howard
Paisley

ETON MESS

Serves 4

2	Egg whites
100g	Caster sugar
350g	Blackberries
100g	Raspberries
	Handful of blueberries
50g	Caster sugar
1	Vanilla pod, split or few
	drops vanilla extract
300ml	Whipping cream

Preheat the oven to 120°C. ❶ For the meringues, whisk egg whites in a bowl until stiff. Add half the caster sugar and beat until incorporated, then beat in the remainder until stiff and glossy. ❷ Spoon onto a baking tray lined with parchment paper, bake in preheated over for 2 hours, then switch off and leave to cool in oven. ❸ Place blackberries and caster sugar in a small pan and heat gently until berries soften. Crush berries lightly with a fork and leave to cool. ❹ Add vanilla seeds or extract to the cream and whip to soft peaks. Fold in approximately ⅔ of the blackberries. Break the meringues into pieces and fold into the blackberry cream, reserving some. ❺ To serve, place some of the blackberry cream onto plates or glass cups, sprinkle over some raspberries and blueberries, another serving of the cream, rest of broken meringues and more loose berries. ❻ Drizzle over the blackberry syrup and serve.

Sharmi Musgrave
Buchanan Castle, Drymen

RHUBARB MERINGUE TART

1	Sheet shortcrust pastry
800g	Rhubarb, cut into 3cm pieces
1	Orange, zested
3 tbsp	Caster sugar

Meringue:

2	Egg whites
100g	Caster sugar
	Double cream to serve

Preheat the oven to 200°C/Fan 180°C/Gas Mark 6. ❶ Line an 8 inch loose-bottomed flan tin with the pastry. Prick the base with a fork, line with greaseproof paper and fill with baking beans. Blind-bake for 15 minutes, remove the paper and beans, then cook for a further 5 minutes to lightly brown. Set aside. ❷ Turn the oven down to 180°C/Fan 160°C/Gas Mark 4. ❸ Put the rhubarb, orange zest and caster sugar in a pan. ❹ Cook for 5-6 minutes until the rhubarb is just starting to soften. ❺ Strain through a sieve and save the excess juice. ❻ Whisk the egg whites in a clean bowl until stiff peaks are formed, then gradually add the caster sugar, whisking in a little at a time. ❼ Put the rhubarb in the pastry case and top with the meringue mixture. Bake for 20 minutes. Serve with double cream or ice cream and drizzle the remaining juices over the top.

Lynn Murray
Buchanan Castle, Drymen

NATURAL YOGHURT WITH STEWED PRUNES

	Dried prunes
1 dsp	Molasses
	Yoghurt

❶ Place dried prunes into pan, cover with water and add a dessert spoon of molasses, bring to boil and allow to cool. ❷ Keep in fridge for a week and use 2-3 a day on top of your yoghurt. I also put this on top of porridge or muesli.

Molasses is one of the best foods rich in iron that is easily absorbed by the body. A very simple yet delicious start or end to the day.

Mary Laidlaw
Lochwinnoch

CAMILLA'S CHOCOLATE MOUSSE

8oz Plain chocolate
2 tbsp Water
1oz Butter, softened
4 Eggs, separated

❶ Boil a pan of water, place a bowl over the top of the pan, making sure it does not touch the water and place the chocolate chunks in the bowl until they melt. ❷ Remove from the heat and beat in the butter. ❸ Add the water, the mixture should now look glossy; add the egg yolks, 1 at a time. ❹ In another bowl, whisk up the egg whites until stiff, fold the egg whites into the chocolate mixture and then spoon into serving bowls. Pour into dishes and leave in the fridge overnight.

Warning. This recipe contains raw eggs.

Camilla Guthrie
Bearsden

ELLE'S CHOCOLATE DELIGHT

85g	Butter
2 tbsp	Golden syrup
2 tbsp	Cocoa powder
170g	Digestives, crushed
175g	Bag Maltesers, half crushed and half left whole

❶ Melt the butter and golden syrup in a small heavy base saucepan. Add in the cocoa powder digestives and crushed Maltesers. ❷ Stir until well combined. ❸ Allow to cool, and then stir through the whole Maltesers. ❹ Line a 1lb loaf tin with cling film, pour in the mixture and press down well, but be careful not to crush the whole Maltesers. ❺ Chill until set (you can put it in the fridge) for about 2 hours. ❻ Cut into chunky fingers and serve.

Cameron, June and Elle McCann
Ealain Gallery, Drymen

FUDGE CAKES

½lb **Biscuits**
**Few sultanas or cherries,
chopped (optional)**
¼lb **Sugar**
¼lb **Margarine or butter**
1 **Small tin of condensed milk**
7 sq **Chocolate**

❶ Melt margarine, sugar and milk. ❷ Add crushed biscuits and fruit if using. Leave to cool. ❸ Melt 7 squares of Scot chocolate over pan of hot water. Pour over mixture and leave to set. Cut into squares or fingers.

Peggy Walker, a friend of my mother gave me this recipe when the children were young. They loved it!

Sheila

CONTINENTAL SLICE

2 cups **Wheatmeal biscuits, crushed**
¼lb **Butter**
1 **Egg**
½ cup **Sugar**
1 cup **Coconut**
1½ **Cocoa**
1 cup **Walnuts, finely chopped**

First topping:

¼lb **Butter**
2 cups **Icing sugar**
2 tbsp **Custard powder**
2 tbsp **Hot water**

Second topping:

4oz **Chocolate bits**
2oz **Butter**

❶ Melt butter and sugar and beaten egg together over hot water until sugar has dissolved then add crushed biscuits and coconut, cocoa and nuts. Press into a swiss roll tin and place in fridge until set. ❷ Beat together the ingredients for the first topping, spread over the biscuit base and put in the fridge to set. ❸ Melt together the ingredients for the second topping and pour over and allow to set. Leave in fridge until ready to eat.

Lynne McMillan
Glasgow

DAFFODIL CREAM

½lb	Caster sugar
3	Eggs, separated
½ tsp	Lemon zest
2 tbsp	Lemon juice
1	Large tin of pineapples, cut into very small pieces
½ pt	Evaporated milk
½ pt	Pineapple juice
½oz	Gelatine (mix with 3 tbsp hot, not boiling water)

❶ Mix sugar, egg yolks, lemon zest and lemon juice together in a bowl.
❷ Add pineapple, whipped milk, melted gelatine and pineapple juice.
❸ Add whipped stiff egg whites. Mix all together and leave overnight to set.
Top with whipped cream and decorate to choice.

Light, sweet and delicious!

Frances Lander

MABEL'S CHOCOLATE MOUSSE

6	Large eggs
1½	Blocks of cooking chocolate
250ml	Double cream
1 tsp	Rum essence (optional)
	Orange segments (optional)

❶ Place the chocolate in a bowl and melt gently over simmering hot water.
❷ Separate the white from the yolks and whisk until firm. Switch the yolks.
Mix the cream until stiff (not too stiff). ❸ Once chocolate has melted: Add the
yolks to the melted chocolate. ❹ Add egg whites. ❺ Fold in cream. ❻ Add rum
essence if required.

Once smooth, pour into dish and leave to set in the fridge. Decorate with orange
segments if required.

Isabell Cameron
Drymen

CHOCOLATE SAUCE

8oz Dark chocolate
2 dsp Water
6oz Caster sugar
½ pt Double cream
A drop or 2 of liqueur
of choice

❶ Break the chocolate into small pieces and put it into a small saucepan with 2 dessert spoons of water. ❷ Heat it very gently, stirring it occasionally until the chocolate has melted into a smooth cream. ❸ Stir in the sugar and cream and bring the sauce to the boil. ❹ Take off the heat and stir in liqueur of choice. (This can be omitted if preferred). Pour into a sauceboat, and serve hot or cold. Hot with ice-cream is delicious! This sauce also goes well with profiteroles.

Betty Beith
Buchanan Castle, Drymen

RUMTOPF
RUM POT

Fresh fruit (non bruised)
Strawberries, peeled and
quartered
Raspberries, peeled and
quartered
Blackberries, peeled and
quartered
Peaches, peeled and
quartered
Apricots, halved
Pears, halved
Good quality dark rum
Sugar

❶ Add a layer of fruit, some sugar and then the rum, covering the fruit.
❷ Adding more fruit, sugar and rum throughout the summer. ❸ Keep in a
cool place and shake or stir gently from time to time and top up with more
rum if needed. Absolutely delicious!

A delicious dish from Germany. Soft summer fruit is used as it comes into
season and added every so often. This can be repeated throughout the
summer. Very easy to prepare, as there is no cooking. It will keep for months
and is very warming to eat during winter. You will also need an airtight container,
either glass or glazed pottery.

Wilma Murray
Milngavie

CELEBRITY

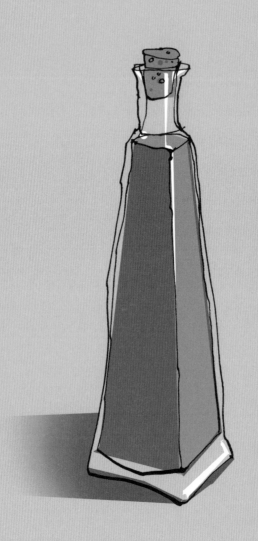

PAO DE QUEIJO' (CHEESE BREADS)

Makes 20 rolls

2 cups	Sweet manioc starch/ tapioca
1 cup	Milk
½ cup	Margarine or butter
1 tsp	Salt
1½ cups	(200g) Parmesan cheese, grated
2	Eggs

Preheat oven to 350°F. ❶ Put the milk, salt, and margarine in a pot and bring to the boil. Remove from heat. ❷ Add hot liquid to the manioc starch, stirring constantly until thoroughly mixed and then allow to cool. ❸ Add the cheese and eggs. Knead (by hand or in a mixer) until you have a soft smooth consistency. ❹ Form into small balls approximately 2 inches in diameter and place on a greased baking sheet. ❺ Let sit for half an hour. ❻ Sprinkle with Parmesan cheese. ❼ Bake for 25 minutes until golden brown. Eat while hot.

I couldn't stop guzzling this cheese bread during a University year in Brazil.

Karen Greenshields
Reporter, Team STV

FILO PASTRY PARCELS WITH PARMA HAM AND FIGS

Makes 4 parcels

Filo pastry (ready-made)
Butter
4 Slices of Parma ham
Dolcelatte cheese
6 Fresh figs (dried and soaked in hot water would do)
Golden syrup

❶ First peel the figs, cut into quarters and scoop into a bowl. Drizzle liberally with syrup, enough to coat the figs. Set to one side. ❷ Next take your Parma ham, separate the slices and lay out on board ready to make up the parcels. ❸ Cut the Dolcelatte cheese into thick cubes about an inch long and the same thickness. ❹ Place them at 1 end of the Parma ham slice, scoop around 2 teaspoons of the fig mixture and roll up into a parcel. ❺ Then take a large knob of butter (2 tablespoons) and gently melt in a pan. ❻ Take the filo pastry and carefully peel back 3 thin sheets and cut into a large square, approximately 10cm^2. Brush liberally with butter on both sides (make sure your filo pastry has been kept in a moist towel otherwise it can be very delicate to handle and break up easily). ❼ Place the ham parcel in the centre of the pastry square. ❽ Pull one tip of the pastry over to meet the other making a triangle shape then pinch round the edges and brush with more butter. Repeat the same process with each ham parcel. ❾ Place on a greased oven tray and cook at 200°C for 15 minutes or until you can see the filo has gone crisp and golden.

Debi Edward
Team STV

FILO PASTRY PARCELS WITH BLACK PUDDING FILLING

Makes 4 parcels

Filo pastry (ready-made)
Butter
2 Slices black pudding
2 Cooking apples
Raisins
White wine vinegar
Scottish Whisky (Famous Grouse or similar)
Demerara sugar
1 Large sprig of rosemary

❶ Peel and dice 2 large cooking apples and place in a pan over a medium heat with 2 tablespoons of water and 2 tablespoons of brown sugar. Sprinkle in a handful of raisins, 2 teaspoons of white wine vinegar and a measure of Whisky. Place a sprig of rosemary on the top (keep it whole so it can be removed later) and then put the lid on. It should just take 10 minutes or so for the apple to soften down into a chunky purée. ❷ Take the pan off the heat and set to one side. ❸ Next take your black pudding, remove the paper from round the edges and cut in half. ❹ Prepare the filo as on previous page and then prepare to make up the parcels. ❺ Place the black pudding in the centre of the square crumbling it slightly then spoon over a good dollop of the apple mix (having removed the rosemary sprig). ❻ Fold over into a triangle, brush with butter, repeat until you have 4 perfect parcels and then cook on a greased tray at 200°C for 15 minutes or until you see the filo has gone crisp and golden.

Ideal as a starter/light lunch served with rocket leaves and a balsamic dressing or made in a bite size form as a canapé.

Debi Edward
Team STV

CULLEN SKINK

2	Medium smoked haddock or Finnan haddock or 1 large haddock on the bone
2	Medium onions
1 pt	Milk
1 lb	Potatoes
2 oz	Butter

❶ Put fish in cold water, enough to cover. Bring to the boil and simmer for 10 minutes. ❷ Take out fish and remove bones and skin. Flake fish. ❸ Cook onion in the 2oz of butter, taking care not to brown the onion. ❹ Cook potatoes and mash with a knob of butter. ❺ Add liquid from fish, pint of milk and onion. Salt, pepper and a small amount of parsley may be added to taste.

Alex Salmond
First Minister

MRS KELLY'S FAMOUS SOUP

2	Pieces of uncooked chicken (legs are best)
4-5	Carrots
1	Small turnip
4	Potatoes
1	Large leek
4	Sticks of celery
	Parsley

❶ Put the chicken pieces in a pot. Cover with water and cook. (Don't use too much water, you can always add more later if you need to). ❷ Chop up the carrots, turnip, potatoes, leek and celery. (Chop up the leek and celery finer than the other chunks, making sure the celery isn't 'stringy'). ❸ Put the veg in the pot with the chicken and water as you cut them up. ❹ Bring to the boil, reduce heat and simmer for 1 hour. ❺ Add salt and pepper to taste. ❻ When the vegetables are ready (just taste it and you will know when it is soft enough) take the chicken pieces out and mash the vegetables. ❼ Skin the chicken, chop it up and put the pieces back in the pot. Finally chop up and add the parsley.

This is the recipe for my mum's famous chicken soup. It is healthy, tasty and cheap and is the ultimate comfort food. My mum is called Anne Kelly and she is 66 and from Glasgow

Lorraine Kelly
TV Presenter

HOMEMADE TOMATO SOUP

1 Large onion
1 Rasher unsmoked
  back bacon
1 Carrot
1 Medium potato
1½ pt Stock (vegetable or
  chicken)
1 Tin of chopped tomatoes
1 Bouquet garni
¼ pt Single cream

❶ Chop and fry the onion, bacon, carrot and potato in 1 tablespoon of oil for 5-10 minutes until soft. ❷ Transfer to large pot and add the stock, chopped tomatoes and bouquet garni. ❸ Remove bouquet garni and blend the soup mixture. ❹ Add ¼ pint of single cream and heat gently for 2-3 minutes. Serve with plenty of ground black pepper.

Don't forget to remove the bouquet garni!

There's nothing like a healthy, home-made soup to banish those winter blues!

Heather Reid
Senior Broadcast Meteorologist, BBC

LENTIL SOUP

6	Rashers of smoked streaky bacon, rind removed and finely chopped	8oz	(225g) Tin of Italian tomatoes
6oz	(175g), Green-brown lentils, washed and drained	2	Garlic cloves, peeled and crushed
1 tbsp	Oil	3 pts	(1¾ litres) Home-made stock
2	Carrots, chopped	8oz	(225g) Cabbage, finely shredded
2	Medium onions, peeled and chopped	2 tbsp	Fresh parsley, chopped
2	Celery stalks, sliced		Salt and pepper

❶ Heat the oil in a large cooking pot and fry the bacon in it until the fat begins to run. ❷ Then stir in the prepared carrots, onion and celery and, with the heat fairly high, toss them around to brown them a little at the edges. ❸ Now stir in the washed, drained lentils, tomatoes and the crushed garlic. ❹ Then add the stock. ❺ As soon as the soup comes to the boil, put a lid on and simmer, as gently as possible, for about 1 hour. ❻ About 15 minutes before the end add the cabbage. Taste and season. Just before serving stir in the chopped parsley.

Nicola Sturgeon
Deputy First Minister

SWEET POTATO AND COCONUT SOUP

3 Sweet potatoes
1 Large onion
2 Garlic cloves
1 Tin of coconut milk
3 Vegetable or chicken
  stock cubes
  Fresh coriander

❶ Chop and panfry the garlic and onion. ❷ Peel and dice the sweet potatoes and add, allowing to sweat for 10 minutes, stirring continuously, so as not to burn. ❸ Add the stock, and allow to simmer for 30 minutes on low heat, (or until ingredients are soft). ❹ Liquidise with a hand blender and add coconut milk and chopped coriander.

My daughter, Christie made this at her 12th birthday cookery party, and later was a bestselling fundraiser at her school.

Carol Smillie
TV Presenter

ROAST SHELLFISH SPAGHETTI WITH LEMON, GARLIC AND PARSLEY BUTTER

Serves 2

1lb	Lobster, split and claws, cracked
2	Large handfuls of rope mussels, cleaned and scrubbed
6	Medium fresh scallops (ideally hand dived)
6	King prawns, shelled and de-veined
2	Handfuls of cooked spaghetti
1	Large handful of flat leaf parsley, coarsely chopped
1	Large lemon, juiced and zested
¾	Garlic cloves, finely chopped
½ tbsp	Good olive oil
2 tbsp	Butter
	Salt and pepper

Preheat oven to its hottest setting. ❶ Evenly arrange all shellfish on roasting tray, sprinkle with olive oil to coat shellfish, season with salt and pepper to taste and roast in oven for 12-15 minute until nicely browned. ❷ In large frypan or wok (big enough to take shellfish but can be done in 2 batches) heat butter, garlic and zest until butter begins to brown around edges. ❸ To pan or wok add pasta, parsley, lemon juice, shellfish and roasting juices toss to incorporate shellfish, adjust seasoning and serve with salad and crusty bread.

John Quigley, Chef
Red Onion Restaurant Glasgow

MARINATED STIR FRY SHETLAND LAMB

1lb	Shetland lamb, cut into cubes
1½ tbsp	Oil for frying
¼ pt	Chicken stock
4oz	Cabbage, shredded
2 tbsp	Stem ginger or ¼ tsp ground ginger

Marinade:

3 tbsp	Soy sauce
2 tbsp	Wine vinegar
2 tbsp	Brown sugar
1	Garlic clove, crushed

❶ Mix lamb into marinade ingredients and leave for at least 2 hours. ❷ Heat half of the oil in pan and stir fry lamb for 5-8 minutes. ❸ Add stock and cook for further 5 minutes. Remove lamb and keep warm. ❹ Heat remaining oil and stir fry cabbage and ginger for 2-3 minutes. ❺ Stir the lamb into vegetables and serve.

Tavish Scott
MSP

SUE LAWRENCE'S HAGGIS LASAGNE

1	Large (approximately 900g/2lb) haggis
250g	(9oz) Sheets pre-cooked lasagne
3-4	Large ripe tomatoes, sliced
40g	(1½oz) Butter
40g	(1½oz) Plain flour
500ml	(18fl oz) Milk
3 tbsp	Parmesan cheese, freshly grated
	Olive oil

❶ Cut open the haggis and crumble with your fingers. Scatter some over the base of a buttered lasagne dish. ❷ Top with a third of the lasagne sheets then top with more haggis. ❸ Top with the tomatoes, season well, top with lasagne and the remaining haggis, then remaining lasagne. ❹ For the sauce, melt the butter, add the flour, stirring to form a roux then gradually add the milk, stirring or whisking to form a sauce. ❺ Stir for 4-5 minutes then season to taste. ❻ Pour this over the remaining lasagne, top with the cheese and a drizzle of oil. ❼ Bake, uncovered, at 180°C/350°F/Gas Mark 4 for 50-55 minutes, or until golden and the lasagne soft. (Check with the tip of a knife). Rest for 10 minutes or so before cutting.

Sue Lawrence
Masterchef Winner

MONKFISH IN CHILLI CASSEROLE

Serves 4

3lbs	Monkfish
2lbs	Tomatoes, skinned, seeded and chopped
4	Onions, finely chopped
4 tbsp	Olive oil
3 tsp	Chilli powder
3	Fresh chillies, chopped
2 tsp	Salt
2	Garlic clove
	Basmati rice

❶ Use hob to oven casserole dish if possible. ❷ Add oil to pan. Sauté onions, garlic, chilli powder, chillies and peppers (if desired) until golden. ❸ Add strips of monkfish. ❹ Cover with tomatoes. Add salt. ❺ Cover dish and cook at 190°C for 20 minutes. ❻ Remove lid and cook for a further 5 minutes. ❼ Serve with basmati rice.

Elaine C. Smith
Actress

LOUISE'S FRIDAY NIGHT CURRY

Serves 4

3-4	Chicken breasts, cut into strips
1	Onion
1	Red chilli, deseeded and finely chopped (wear thin rubber disposable gloves)
	Garam masala (Supermarket bought)
	Paprika
4	Garlic cloves
5cm	Piece of root ginger, half finely grated and the rest cut into long thin strips

4 tbsp	Tomato puree,
	Coconut milk or double cream
1	Lemon, juiced
	Nut or olive oil
25g	Butter
25g	Light brown sugar
	Warm, previously boiled water
	Salt
	Large sprig of coriander, washed and chopped
	Sliced blanched almonds

❶ Sauté the chicken strips in a frying pan until thoroughly cooked. ❷ While this is cooking, place the chopped onion, 4 crushed garlic cloves, the grated ginger, lemon juice, 2 tablespoons of oil, 1 teaspoon of paprika, 2 teaspoons of garam masala and the chopped chilli and give it all a whiz in a good blender. You may want to add a few tablespoons of water to help bind the ingredients. Pulse until it forms a paste. ❸ In a separate frying/sauté pan, melt the butter and add the fresh paste. Mix and cook gently until the butter begins to separate from the paste. ❹ Meanwhile, add the tomato puree to a measuring jug along with the sugar and a pinch of salt and add 250ml of warm, recently boiled water. Cover with lid or tinfoil lid and cook gently for 10 minutes. ❺ Check chicken which should have cooked through by now. Set chicken aside. ❻ Once the above has cooked for 20 minutes, add either the 250ml of double cream or ¾ of the coconut milk (discard the rest) and the strips of ginger. Stir and then add the chicken strips and some coriander. Cover and cook for 20 minutes, stirring occasionally. ❼ Serve with coriander, almonds and a sprinkling of garam masala over the top of the curry and the usual rice, naan etc. I love it with a dollop of mango chutney.

Louise White
Team STV

SUPREME OF CHICKEN DUNVEGAN WITH WILD RICE

Serves 4

4 **Chicken fillets**
Salt and pepper

Sauce:

400g **Wild mushrooms, sliced**
1 **Small onion, diced**
1 **Garlic clove, finely chopped**
100ml **Pinot Grigio wine**
¾ pt **Double Cream**
½ **Chicken stock cube**
1 tbsp **Olive oil**

Rice:

1 pt **Cold water**
½ pt **Wild rice**
Pinch of salt

Flat leaf parsley, chopped

❶ Place chicken fillets in an oven tray and cover with water. Season and cook for 20 minutes at 200°C. ❷ Sauce: Heat oil in a pan, add mushrooms, onion and garlic and fry until lightly browned. ❸ Add wine and reduce by half. Add cream and stock cube and gently simmer for 5 minutes and set aside. ❹ Rice: Put cold water in a pot, add rice and salt. Cover with a lid and bring to the boil. Turn off heat when the water starts to boil and leave to stand for 10 minutes, with the lid remaining on. All the water will be completely absorbed by the rice. ❺ Serve rice on plates directly from the pot, add the cooked chicken and pour the sauce over. Add some parsley and enjoy!

Murdo MacLeod
Ex Scotland and Celtic F.C. Footballer

MUM'S MOUSSAKA

A few handfuls of chopped lamb (Sunday roast leftovers work best)
1 Onion, chopped
3-4oz Butter
3-4 tbsp Tomato sauce
Salt and pepper
1 Garlic clove, crushed
Pinch grated nutmeg
2 Tins of tomatoes
1 Aubergine
2-3 Potatoes

Béchamel sauce:

3-4 oz Butter
1 tbsp Flour
7½fl oz Milk
Slice of onion
Couple of peppercorns
2-3 Parsley stalks (don't worry if you leave these out)
Little mustard
1 Egg, separated
Grated cheese, a few handfuls

❶ Slice aubergine and sprinkle with salt. Leave for a few hours to draw out moisture. ❷ Boil potatoes until they're cooked but not overdone. ❸ While the potatoes are boiling, prepare the filling: Soften the onion in butter (keep 1 slice of onion for the sauce). Add lamb. Add all other ingredients for filling apart from potatoes and aubergine. Leave to simmer. ❹ When the potatoes are done, drain and set aside. Slice when cooled. ❺ Wash salt off the aubergines and lightly fry in a little oil (griddle pan, or frying pan is fine.) ❻ Use large deep dish and fill with layers of aubergine, then potato, then meat filling. Having as many, or few layers as you like. Finish off with a layer of either potato, aubergine or both on the top. Remember to leave room for your sauce on top! ❼ Béchamel sauce: Whisk egg white until it's fluffy and forming peaks, set aside. ❽ Melt butter and quickly stir in the flour. Slowly add milk, stirring all the time. Add onion slice, peppercorns, parsley and mustard. Beat in the egg yolk and a little cheese. Finally fold in your egg white. You should have a cheese sauce which is a bit fluffier than normal. ❾ Pour over your layers of potato, aubergine and meat. Sprinkle with remaining cheese. Bake for 15-30 minutes (Gas Mark 6) until cheese on top has browned slightly. Eat and marvel at how yummy it is!

Eleanor Bradford
Health Correspondent, BBC Scotland

CREAMY CHICKEN

Serves 4

- 1 Knob of butter
- 1 Large onion, chopped finely
- ½ pt Chicken stock
- 4 Chicken breasts, cut into strips
- ½ Carton of double cream

❶ Melt butter in large pan, add the onion and fry for a couple of minutes. ❷ Add the chicken and cook on all sides. ❸ Add the chicken stock and simmer for 20 minutes. ❹ Take off the heat and slowly add cream stirring slowly. Add salt and pepper to taste. If necessary, to thicken add McDougals granules. Best served immediately. Serve with a pasta of your choice: we like it with spaghetti.

This recipe makes a fantastic base for a creamy curry by adding curry spices to taste.

This is a family recipe which we love and our children ask for it frequently especially when they have friends over for dinner.

Ford Kiernan and Lesley Kiernan
Actor

VENISON STEAKS WITH A RASPBERRY DRESSING, TOMATO AND HAGGIS STACK

10ml	Scottish rapeseed oil
2 x 100g	Venison steaks
4	Scottish tomatoes, sliced
300g	Haggis, sliced in 4
100g	Kale, washed and shredded
	A dash of Benromach Speyside Single Malt Whisky
4	Medium potatoes, peeled and cut in a small dice
	Salt and pepper
	A drizzle of raspberry vinegar

Preheat oven to 190°C. ❶ Cut rounds of tomato and circles of haggis. Place a slice of haggis on a foil lined baking tray. Add a layer of sliced tomato. Repeat to form a stack. ❷ Cook for 15 minutes to thoroughly heat through. When cooked, add a dash of whisky and keep warm. ❸ Meanwhile brush venison with oil and season with pepper. ❹ Heat a heavy frying pan and sear venison on a high heat for a couple of minutes. Reduce heat and cook for 3 more minutes. Turn over steaks and cook for a further 6 minutes for medium cooked steaks. ❺ Place steaks on a warmed plate and cover loosely with foil. Allow to rest for 10 minutes. ❻ Meanwhile add potatoes to pan with a drizzle of the rapeseed oil to loosen the tasty venison residues and toss frequently to cook through. ❼ Whilst the potatoes are cooking, cook kale in boiling lightly salted water for 5 minutes then drain. (Toss in a little local butter if wished!). ❽ To serve, place a spoonful of kale in the dish. Slice venison and set on top of kale. Lift haggis stack onto plate, add a spoonful of potato and finish with a generous drizzle of raspberry vinegar. Serve immediately.

Richard Lochhead (MSP)
This recipe has been provided by Wendy Barrie who is a cookery show presenter throughout Britain and is director of the award-winning www.scottishfoodguide.com

RASPBERRY VINEGAR

Makes 400ml

250ml **White wine vinegar**
1 **Punnet raspberries**
300g **Caster sugar***

❶ Pour vinegar into a measuring jug and top up with raspberries to reach 500ml. ❷ Mash gently – potato masher is ideal fit in the jug. ❸ Leave for a couple of days, minimum overnight, and mash once more. ❹ Strain through a sieve into a bowl then back into jug to measure liquid. ❺ Place vinegar and sugar in a pan. Dissolve and simmer for 10 minutes until syrupy. ❻ Pour into warmed sterilized bottles and seal.

*This quantity of sugar is based on my liquid measuring 400ml so add proportionately more as necessary.

Richard Lochhead (MSP)
This recipe has been provided by Wendy Barrie who is a cookery show presenter throughout Britain and is director of the award-winning www.scottishfoodguide.com

CARAMELISED ONION, ROCKET AND GOAT'S CHEESE TARTLETS

300g	Shortcrust pastry flour (for dusting)
25g	Unsalted butter
6	Large onions, peeled and thinly sliced
1 tbsp	Sherry vinegar
150g	Goat's cheese, preferably a thin log
100g	Rocket
	Squeeze of lemon juice
	Drizzle of olive oil
	Salt and pepper

❶ Cut the pastry into 4 even pieces and roll each out on a lightly floured board as thinly as possible, without tearing. Use to line 4 x 10cm tartlet tins and leave the excess pastry overhanging the sides. ❷ Place tartlets on a baking sheet and line with foil and baking beans. Chill for at least 20 minutes. ❸ Preheat oven to 200°C/Gas Mark 6. Bake pastry cases for 15 minutes, then remove baking beans and foil and return to the oven for another 5 minutes until the pastry is crisp. ❹ While still hot, trim the pastry to the rim of the tins with a sharp knife. Cool on a wire rack. ❺ Meanwhile, heat the butter in a pan and add sliced onions. Cook over a very low heat for about 30 minutes, stirring occasionally, until the onions are very soft and caramelised. ❻ Drain off any excess liquid from the onions and add the sherry vinegar. Put the pan back on the heat for 10 more minutes until the vinegar has cooked off. Season well and leave to cool. ❼ Heat the oven to 200°C/Gas Mark 6. Place the tartlet cases on a baking sheet and spoon in the caramelised onions. ❽ Cut the goat's cheese into 8 thick slices and place 2 on each tartlet. Bake for 5-10 minutes until the cheese is golden and the tart has warmed through. ❾ Dress the rocket with lemon juice, olive oil, salt and black pepper and serve with the warm tartlets.

Gordon Ramsay
Chef

RISOTTO WITH PRAWN, LEMON, SPRING ONION AND BASIL

	Olive oil
½	Onion, finely chopped
1	Garlic clove, finely chopped
150g	Risotto rice
75ml	White wine
750ml	Warm light vegetable stock

	Bunch of spring onions, thinly sliced
150g	Cooked peeled prawns
3 tbsp	Low-fat crème fraîche
	Squeeze of lemon
½	Bunch of basil, chopped
	Salt and pepper

❶ Heat splash of oil, gently fry onion and garlic until they become translucent. ❷ Add rice, continue frying for 2 minutes. ❸ Add wine, stir until wine is absorbed. ❹ Add stock, ladle by ladle, stirring until stock is absorbed between each spoonful. Give risotto lots of tender, loving care, by stirring regularly, and the creamy starch will come out of each grain. Continue like this for 10-15 minutes. ❺ Add spring onion to risotto, continue cooking for 5 minutes, then add prawns and crème fraîche. ❻ Now this is the important point. Rice needs to be al dente, so keep tasting it until it's time to take it off the heat (probably need another 5 minutes). ❼ Add a squeeze of lemon and stir through basil. Check seasoning and grate some lemon zest over the top.

Kaye Adams
TV Presenter

COD, PRAWN AND COCONUT CURRY

Serves 4

1 fl oz	Light olive oil	¾ pt	Coconut milk
1 oz	Salted butter	¼ oz	Fresh ground pepper
4	Shallots, peeled and sliced lengthways	½ oz	Maldon sea salt flakes
2	Medium garlic cloves, peeled and finely sliced	2 oz	Fresh coriander leaves, roughly chopped
10	Fresh curry leaves	2	Limes, zested and quartered
4	Small green fresh chillies and seeds, finely chopped	1	Fresh mango, stoned and evenly sliced
1 oz	Coriander powder	8	Large tiger prawns, cooked and peeled
½ oz	Turmeric	1 lb	Thick fresh cod fillet, skin off, cut into large pieces
1 oz	Black mustard seeds	4	Servings of Basmati rice
1 fl oz	Nam pla (fish sauce)		

❶ Heat oil and butter in thick based pan and add leaves, mustard seeds until lightly coloured. ❷ Add shallots, garlic and chillies until soft. ❸ Add pepper, salt, turmeric, coriander powder and mango. ❹ Add Nam pla then blend into mixture until loose. ❺ Add coconut milk, prawns and lime zest. Gently simmer with lid on for 20 minutes. ❻ Cook the rice so that it is light and fluffy. Once cooked keep hot under cling film. ❼ Add cod and cook gently without lid until tender but so its not breaking up. ❽ Plate rice onto hot plates and spoon on curry. ❾ Garnish with fresh coriander and limes.

This is a gloriously delicate and fragrant dish with subtle Indian overtones but without anaesthetising the palette.

Laurie Mill
Chef 4U

ROASTED SALMON AND VEGETABLES WITH A BALSAMIC DRESSING

2	Salmon fillets
12	Cherry tomatoes
1	Large red onion
1	Yellow pepper
1	Red pepper
1	Punnet button mushrooms
1 tbsp	Olive oil
1-2 tbsp	Balsamic vinegar
	Freshly ground black pepper

Preheat the oven to 180°C. ❶ Add the salmon, onion, mushrooms and peppers to a preheated baking tray. ❷ Pour the olive oil and balsamic vinegar over the contents, stirring to coat evenly. ❸ Bake for 10 minutes, then remove and add the cherry tomatoes. ❹ Bake for a further 5-10 minutes or until the fish is cooked through. ❺ Add freshly ground black pepper to taste, serve and enjoy!

This super simple recipe tastes great and is also a wonderful source of omega 3 from the salmon.

Patrick Holford
zest4life

CHILLI MARINATED STEAK

Serves 4

4 x 120g	Beef steaks, rump or sirloin
1 tbsp	Cider vinegar
1	Garlic clove, crushed
1	Red chilli, finely sliced
1 tbsp	Grainy mustard
1 tbsp	Fresh mint, chopped
1 tbsp	Fresh parsley, chopped
	Salt and pepper

❶ Season the steaks on both sides with salt and black pepper. ❷ Place the marinade ingredients in a bowl and mix well. Add the steaks, coating them on all sides. Cover and chill in the refrigerator until required. ❸ Remove the steaks from the refrigerator 30 minutes before cooking. ❹ 5 minutes before cooking, preheat a health grill or conventional grill. ❺ Cook the steaks for 5 minutes in the health grill or 10-12 minutes on each side under a conventional grill, or to your taste.

Here's a tip for a fuller flavour, leave the steaks to marinate for up to 3 days

Preperation time: 5 minutes and 20 minutes cook time
Per serving: 175 calories. 7.7g fat

Rosemary Conley's
Slim to Win

GRIDDLED SALMON WITH GARLIC AND BASIL WHITE BEANS

Serves 4

4	Fillets salmon (125g each)	420g	Tin of cannellini white beans, drained
2-3 tbsp	Extra virgin olive oil		
1	Lemon, cut in wedges	1 small	Knob of butter or 1 tbsp crème fraîche
1	Small onion, sliced thinly		
1	Fat garlic clove, crushed	6	Large leaves fresh basil, torn in strips
2	Tomatoes, skinned and chopped roughly		Salt and pepper

❶ Brush the salmon fillets with half the oil, season lightly and cook either in a preheated ridged iron griddle for about 3-5 minutes on each side or under a preheated grill. The fish is cooked when it feels firm. ❷ Remove and squeeze over a little lemon juice. Set aside. ❸ Sauté the onion, garlic and chopped tomato in the remaining oil for about 5 minutes until softened then stir in the beans. ❹ Heat until bubbling and cook for a couple of minutes then beat in the butter or crème fraîche, some seasoning and the basil. ❺ Remove from the heat and spoon alongside the salmon to serve.

Fish and beans complement each other very well in a meal. This dish uses a can of cannellini beans in a quick pan-fry sauce. All it needs is some crusty white bread to mop up the delicious juices.

Loyd Grossman
TV Presenter and Chef

ANDY MURRAY'S FAVOURITE GREEK SHEPHERD'S PIE

Serves 4

½lb	Onions
2 tbsp	Oil
1lb	Mince
1 tbsp	Chopped parsley
6oz	Tomatoes
1lb	Potatoes
	Salt and pepper
	White sauce
2 tbsp	Grated cheese

❶ Slice onions thinly and fry gently in oil until soft. ❷ Add mince and chopped parsley after a few minutes, stirring from time to time. ❸ Slice the tomatoes and add to meat and cook gently for 5 minutes. ❹ Peel and slice potatoes thinly. ❺ Butter a round soufflé dish and arrange layers of overlapping potato slices on the bottom. Season and spread a layer of meat and tomatoes, then another layer of potatoes. ❻ Make a thick sauce with butter, flour and milk; season well and stir in 2 tablespoons of grated cheese. Pour over the potatoes and shake dish so the sauce penetrates. ❼ Bake in preheated oven at 180°C/350°F for 1¼ hrs or until potatoes are tender. Serve with Green Salad.

Judy Murray
Dunblane

THAI RED CHICKEN CURRY

Serves 4

400g	Chicken breast fillet strips
1	Red pepper, thinly chopped
100g	Baby sweetcorn, halved long ways
100g	Small mushrooms, don't cut them
100g	Spinach leaves (don't cut them)

Curry base:

2 tbsp	Sunflower oil
1	Large onion, sliced thinly
10cm	Fresh root ginger, peeled and cut into thin matchsticks
2	Garlic gloves, crushed
3 tbsp	Thai red curry paste (heaped)
400g	Tin of coconut milk
2	Limes, juiced
4 tbsp	Thai fish sauce
400ml	Vegetable stock
1 tsp	Light soft brown sugar

❶ For the curry base, heat the oil in a large pan. Add in the onion, ginger and garlic and cook gently for 2 minutes without browning. ❷ Add in the chicken breast fillet strips, cook slowly on a low heat for 3 minutes. ❸ Once the chicken starts to change colour, add in the curry paste and cook slowly stirring every 30 seconds. ❹ Add in the coconut milk, sugar, lime juice, Thai fish sauce and stock and simmer for 4 minutes. ❺ Finally add in the baby sweetcorn, mushrooms and spinach leaves, red pepper and simmer for a further 5-6 minutes. Serve with steamed rice. I like the juice to cover the rice!

Dr. Paul Hurrion
Coach with Padraig Harrington

WRAPPED MONKFISH

Serves 2

2	Monkfish tail fillets (150g/5oz each)
8	Slices of Speck ham (or Parma ham)
1 tbsp	Parsley
1 tbsp	Oregano
6 tbsp	Olive oil
6	Sage leaves
1	Shallot
1 tbsp	Red wine vinegar
1	Glass red wine
300ml	(½ pint) Vegetable stock
	Salt and pepper

❶ Start by finely chopping the parsley and oregano, then mix them together with the olive oil to make the marinade, adding salt and pepper to taste. ❷ Skin the monkfish tails, being very careful to remove all of the membrane, or the fish will take on a rubbery texture when cooked. Place the monkfish in a bowl and cover with the marinade, leave for 20 minutes. ❸ Arrange 4 slices of the Speck ham (or Parma ham) side by side on a work surface and place 3 of the sage leaves along the centre. Place 1 of the marinated fillets on the ham, and roll up the sides to enclose the fish. Repeat with the other fillet and the rest of the ham, and place on a baking tray. Cook in an oven at 200°C/400°F/Gas Mark 6 for 12-15 minutes. ❹ For the sauce, finely chop the shallot and fry in a little oil until soft. Add the vinegar and boil until almost dry, then add the red wine and reduce to about a quarter. Add the stock and reduce by about half. Strain through a sieve and season to taste. ❺ To serve, slice the cooked fillet, arrange the slices on the plate and drizzle with the sauce.

Alison Nicolas
European Solheim Cup Captain 2009

DARREN'S SAUSAGE, BEANS AND MASH

	Pork sausages
1	Tin of Heinz baked beans
1 dsp	Cream
	Salt and pepper
	Potatoes

❶ The sausages have to be big thick pork sausages and I put them under the grill to cook them on both sides. ❷ Heat up the beans obviously Heinz in a pan, and the mash is the most critical part! ❸ I put in a dessert spoon of cream, salt and loads of pepper and mash the potatoes until there are no lumps! I hate lumps in mash so it has to be very smooth.

I'm not a very accomplished cook but whenever I get back from being away, my favourite meal is sausage, beans and mashed potatoes!

Darren Clarke
Golfer

MOIRA MACAULAY'S SHORTBREAD

Makes 20-24 pieces

- 225g (8oz) Slightly salted butter, softened
- 110g (4oz) Caster sugar
- 225g (8oz) Plain flour, sifted
- 150g (5oz) Cornflour, sifted
- Caster sugar (for dredging)

❶ Place the butter and sugar in a mixer or food processor and cream until pale. ❷ Add the flour and cornflour and blend briefly, just until thoroughly combined. ❸ Tip into a buttered 23x33cm/9x13 inch swiss roll tin and, using floured hands, press down so it is level. ❹ Prick it all over with a fork (do this carefully so that you don't disturb the level surface), then bake for 50-60 minutes until it's a uniform pale golden colour all over. Do not let it become golden brown. ❺ Remove from the oven and dredge all over with caster sugar, then cut into squares. Leave for 5 minutes or so, then carefully decant onto a wire rack to cool.

Fred MacAulay
Radio and TV Presenter

MAW BROON'S EASY PEASY ALMOND MACAROONS

1 cup **Ground almonds**
¾ cup **Sugar**
1 **Egg white (be prepared, you might need more depending on egg size)**
½ tsp **Vanilla extract**
Some whole skinned almonds

Preheat oven to 200°C/400°F. ❶ Gradually mix the egg white into the dry ingredients above, until mixture is thick and sticky and shapeable. Depends on the size of the egg so judge as you go along. Each macaroon should be about the size of a walnut. ❷ Put on a baking tray covered in rice paper. ❸ Brush each one with some water. ❹ Put a whole almond on top of each 1. Bake for 15 minutes.

Maw Broon
Maw Broon's But an' Ben Cookbook is published by Waverley Books

SCOTTISH SHORTBREAD

8oz Plain flour
4oz Cornfllour
2oz Caster sugar
2oz Icing sugar
4oz Butter
4oz Margarine
Pinch of salt

❶ Cream butter, margarine and sugar. ❷ Add flour and cornflour. Mix well.
❸ Roll out and bake in baking tin in moderate oven for 50 minutes.

Jo Swinson
MP

CHOCOLATE COOKIES

125g	Unsalted butter, softened
90g	Soft light brown sugar
1	Egg
125g	Chocolate spread
2-3	Drops vanilla extract
90g	Caster sugar
200g	Plain flour
30g	Cocoa powder
	Pinch of salt
½ tsp	Baking powder
150g	Chocolate chips (white or milk)

Preheat oven to 350°F. ❶ Cream butter and both sugars. ❷ Beat in egg, chocolate spread and vanilla extract. ❸ Sieve flour, baking powder, cocoa powder and salt into a bowl. ❹ Add to chocolate mixture and gently mix together. ❺ Stir in chocolate chips. ❻ Place mounds of cookie dough onto baking trays. ❼ Bake for 14 minutes. Remove from oven and leave to set for 2-3 minutes.

Eat and enjoy!

Kaye Adams
TV Presenter

RAVEN GOLD RING CUPCAKES

110g **Unsalted butter**
110g **Caster sugar**
30g **Cocoa powder**
2 **Eggs, whisked**
110g **Flour**

❶ Preheat oven to 180°C. ❷ Cream butter and sugar together and add cocoa powder. ❸ Add egg to mixture, fold in flour and spoon mixture into cases. ❹ Bake for 10 minutes. ❺ Decorate with icing cream. ❻ Finally add golden decorative sprinkles to form a ring shape!

James MacKenzie
'Raven' Children's TV

HEATHER'S MUM'S CAKE

Makes 1 cake

200g Sultanas or raisins
100g Margarine
75g Brown sugar
200g Self raising flour
1 Egg

Preheat oven up to 200°C/Gas Mark 6. ❶ Rub the margarine into the flour in mixing bowl until the mix looks like breadcrumbs. ❷ Mix in the brown sugar, flour and egg. ❸ Line a baking tray with greaseproof paper. ❹ Put small fist size balls of the mix on the tray. ❺ Bake 15-25 minutes (ready when a skewer comes out of cake clean.)

Serve hot from the oven with a cuppa and add lashings of butter. As an alternative to sultanas use coconut – both delicious!

This is my favourite thing to bake on a wet and windy Sunday afternoon. It's my mum's recipe.

Heather Suttie
Real Radio

PERFECT CARROT CAKE

Makes 1 cake

1 cup	Caster sugar
½ cup	Vegetable oil
2	Eggs, beaten
1½ cups	Carrots, grated
1 cup	Flour, unsifted
½ tsp	Salt
1 tsp	Baking soda
1 tsp	Cinnamon
¼ cup	Ground coconut
¼ cup	Nuts
¼ cup	Raisin
1	Mashed up ripe banana (Optional)

Frosting:

200g	Cream cheese, softened
¼ cup	Margarine or butter
2½ cups	Icing sugar

❶ Combine sugar and oil. ❷ Add eggs. Mix well. ❸ Add grated carrots. ❹ Slowly stir in sifted dry ingredients. ❺ Add ground coconut, nuts, and raisins. ❻ Pour batter into lightly greased and floured 9x9 inch square cake pan. ❼ Bake at 200°C/400°F for 20-30 minutes. ❽ Mix together frosting ingredients and when cool, spread frosting over the cake. ❾ Squeeze of lemon and some grated lemon zest.

This is a fool proof and easy American recipe for Carrot Cake using a cup measure (an average sized mug will do if you don't have a cup measure). I usually make double the amount to make 2 x 9x9 inch squares to layer them together with frosting.

Grant Lauchlan
Team STV

SAUTÉED PEACHES WITH LIME, MADEIRA, ALLSPICE AND YOGHURT

Serves 4

2 tbsp	Olive oil
25g	Light muscovado sugar
¼ tsp	Ground nutmeg
¼ tsp	Ground cinnamon
¼ tsp	Allspice (Jamaican pepper)
12	Peach halves (tinned 'cling' variety), in juice or water
50ml	Madeira (can use Sherry)
2 tbsp	Runny honey
2	Large limes, juiced
200g	Thick natural sheep yoghurt

❶ Dry the peaches well using kitchen paper. ❷ Heat the oil, sugar, nutmeg, cinnamon and allspice in a large non-stick frying pan. ❸ Increase the heat and cook until the spices start bubbling. ❹ Add the peaches, cut side down and reduce heat slightly then sauté for about 2 minutes, or until golden brown. Turn peaches over and cook for a further 1-2 minutes. ❺ Pour over the Madeira, honey and the lime juice, and bring together. ❻ To serve, divide the peach halves between 4 bowls, and top with spoonfuls of yoghurt. Pour over the tepid sauce and serve straight away.

Phil Vickery's recipe submitted by Shereen Nanjiani
TV Presenter

ROLLED PAVLOVA

4	Egg whites
200g	Caster sugar
1 tsp	Cornflour
1 tsp	Vinegar
25g	Cinnamon
50g	Flaked almonds
1	Punnet of strawberries
4	Kiwi fruit

❶ Whisk the egg whites until stiff, add half the sugar and whisk again. ❷ Now add the rest of the sugar, cornflour, vinegar and whisk again, until stiff and shiny peaks form. ❸ Lightly oil a Swiss roll tin, cut greaseproof paper to size and lightly oil, dust with cinnamon. Pour in the meringue and smooth out with a spatula, then sprinkle with flaked almonds. ❹ Bake in a preheated oven at 180°C/ 350°F/Gas Mark 4 for approximately 12-15 minutes, until golden brown. ❺ Turn out onto a sheet of greaseproof paper on a wire to cool. ❻ Wash the strawberries and peel the kiwi fruit, reserve 8 strawberries and 8 slices of kiwi fruit for garnish. Chop up the rest of the fruit, not too chunky. ❼ Whip the cream to a soft piping consistency. Spread the cream onto the meringue (on the cinnamon side), now sprinkle the chopped fruit over, and using the paper, roll up like a swiss roll. ❽ Trim the ends, and pipe a rosette of cream per portion and decorate with the reserved fruit.

J H Burgess
Retired from One Devonshire Gardens

BERRY BANANA BAKE

Serves 1

Handful of frozen berries
1 Small bannana
Flaked almonds or nuts
Natural yoghurt or crème
fraîche or ice cream
Shaving of nutmeg or a
vanilla pod

❶ Place a handful of frozen mixed berries into an oven dish. Slice in 1 small banana. ❷ Bake for 15-20 minutes, top with flaked almonds or nuts of your choice and serve with natural yoghurt for the super-healthy option or crème fraîche or ice cream for a slightly more indulgent dessert. You can also shave in some nutmeg or use a vanilla pod.

I was caught short with friends around for dinner one evening and had to create a quick dessert out of what was available. Being a health-conscious type, I wanted taste with no guilt! The result was my 'Berry Banana Bake' which has become a regular favourite – dinner party or not!

Amanda Hamilton
Scottish Nutritionalist and TV Presenter

COCKTAILS

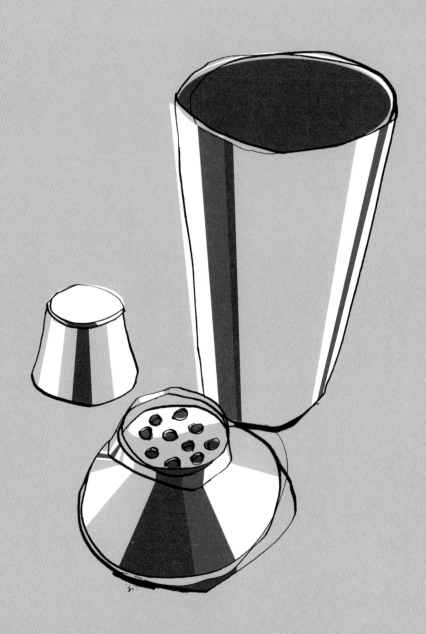

PINK DIVA

3 Strawberries
1 Lime, sliced
Dash of strawberry syrup
Ice, crushed
2 Measures lemon vodka
Split strawberry to decorate

❶ Mix the strawberries, lime and strawberry syrup in a rocks glass and fill it up with crushed ice then add vodka and stir well. ❷ Serve with cocktail stirrer and decorate with split strawberry. Delicious!

PINK WINK

1½ Measures sloe gin
 ½ Measure freshly squeezed
   lemon juice
 ½ Measure sugar syrup
   Ice cubes
   Champagne to top up
   Lemon twist to decorate

❶ Put sloe gin, lemon juice and sugar syrup in cocktail shaker with some ice. Shake well. ❷ Strain into a chilled champagne flute, top up with champagne, stir and decorate with lemon twist. Share with someone special!

PINK PANTHER

3	Ice cubes
100ml	Red wine
25ml	Rum
15ml	Sugar syrup
1 tsp	Orange juice
1 tsp	Lemon juice
	Soda water
1	Lemon slice

❶ Put ice in a tall tumbler with wine, rum, sugar syrup, orange juice and lemon juice. ❷ Stir well and top up with soda water. Fix lemon slice on rim of glass.

Sip and watch the sun set...

PINKY AND PERKY

2-3 Ice cubes
40ml White rum
20ml Red vermouth
1 Cocktail cherry

❶ Crack ice and put into a shaker with rum and vermouth. Shake well and strain into a cocktail glass. ❷ Spear cherry on a cocktail stick and use to decorate.

LEMON SCHNAPPS

Makes 400ml

- 2 **Lemons**
- 70cl **Bottle of vodka**
- 4 **Fresh lime leaves**
  (or Bart Spices freeze
  dried lime leaves)
- 2 tbsp **Caster sugar**

① Carefully pare the zest of 1 lemon in long pieces. Put into a large jar or bowl with a lid. ② Add the vodka, 2 lime leaves and sugar. Cover and store in a cool, dark place for 10 days, to flavour the vodka. ③ Pare the zest from the second lemon and drop it into a 750ml sterilized bottle. ④ Add the remaining lime leaves and strain in the flavoured vodka, removing the solids. Seal and label.

Once opened, chill and use within 1 month. It is delicious served from the freezer!

Lynn Murray

EDINBURGH COSMOPOLITAN

25ml **Citrus vodka**
25ml **Cointreau**
30ml **Cranberry juice**
Dash of lime juice
Dash of lime cordial
Dash of orange bitters
Egg white (optional)

❶ Shake ingredients together in cocktail shaker. ❷ Strain into an iced cocktail glass and garnish with flamed orange segment!

Jane Mathieson
Bearsden

OLD FASHIONED GINGER BEER

½oz	Yeast
	Sugar to feed the plant
7 tsp	Ground ginger
	Sugar to flavour
1 ½lb	Sugar
2	Lemons, juiced

❶ Mix starter ingredients with ¾ pint of warm water in a glass jar. Stir, cover and leave in a warm place for 24 hours. This is your starter 'plant'. Feed the 'plant' with 1 teaspoon each of ground ginger and sugar each day. ❷ After 7 days, strain through a fine sieve. Dissolve the sugar in 2 pints of water. ❸ Add the lemon juice and the liquid from the 'plant'. Dilute with 5 pints of water, mix well and store in corked bottles for at least 7 days. ❹ Use strong bottles as pressure may build up which will cause thin bottles to explode. For the same reason use corked bottles rather than those with a more secure closure that will not 'give' under pressure.

This is a recipe that I have often used and it produces a really old-fashioned drink. It is quite a long process but well worth the effort. The amount of sugar in the final stage can be varied according to taste.

Wilma Murray
Milngavie

FROZEN DAIQUIRIS

1 Part (usually a bottle) of
  white rum
2 Parts Roses (or similar)
  Lime juice
3 Parts water

❶ Mix together in an appropriately-sized plastic container and add a pinch of green food-colouring. ❷ Freeze the mixture in your deep freeze and wait for a hot day. Remove the container a couple of hours before use. ❸ When you can, scoop out an appropriate amount and whiz it up in your blender until it is slushy. Serve with 2 thick straws (as it thaws from the bottom of the glass).

Bruce Nicol
Hastings

THINK PINK SCOTLAND WOULD LIKE TO SAY A BIG **THANK YOU** TO THE FOLLOWING PEOPLE WHO HAVE DONATED THEIR TIME AND EXPERTISE SO GENEROUSLY.

Julie Fraser at Holler PR for her commitment, enthusiasm and wonderful contacts! Maggie, Stuart, Tim and Jodie at Stand Design, Glasgow for their expert advice, fantastic design and dedication to this project pro bono (stand-united.co.uk). To Paul Gray for his fantastic illustrations pro bono (Mr Paul at nbillustration.co.uk). To Nick Thomson at J Thomson Colour Printers for his help and advice, and for contributing to the printing and production of this book. To David Marshall at Borders for instantly agreeing to stock our book. ACA Press Cutters for contributing to the wiro binding. Mark Jennings and Shaun Woods at D8 Digital for their ongoing technical work on the Think Pink Scotland website pro bono (weared8.com). To Lindsey McArthur at University of Glasgow for always being on hand to help! And last but not least a big thank you to the neglected men in our lives for their patience, understanding and help with the grammar and spelling!!!